KWAME NKRUMAH

Consciencism

PHILOSOPHY AND IDEOLOGY
FOR DE-COLONIZATION

MONTHLY REVIEW PRESS

NEW YORK AND LONDON

CONTENTS

AUTHOR'S NOTE

SINCE THE publication of the first edition of *Consciencism* in 1964, the African Revolution has decisively entered a new phase, the phase of armed struggle. In every part of our continent, African revolutionaries are either preparing for armed struggle, or are actively engaged in military operations against the forces of reaction and counter-revolution.

The issues are now clearer than they have ever been. The succession of military coups which have in recent years taken place in Africa, have exposed the close links between the interests of neo-colonialism and the indigenous bourgeoisie. These coups have brought into sharp relief the nature and the extent of the class struggle in Africa. Foreign monopoly capitalists are in close association with local reactionaries, and have made use of officers among the armed forces in order to frustrate the purposes of the African Revolution.

It is in consideration of the new situation in Africa that some changes have become necessary in this edition. They occur principally in Chapter Three.

August 15, 1969
Conakry

According to the materialist conception of history, the *ultimately* determining element in history is the production and reproduction of real life. More than this neither Marx nor I have ever asserted. Hence if somebody twists this into saying that the economic element is the *only* determining one, he transforms that proposition into a meaningless, abstract, senseless phrase. . . . Marx and I are ourselves partly to blame for the fact that the younger people sometimes lay more stress on the economic side than is due to it. We had to emphasize the main principle *vis-à-vis* our adversaries, who denied it, and we had not always the time, the place or the opportunity to allow the other elements involved in the interaction to come into their rights. But when it was a case of presenting a section of history, that is, of a practical application, it was a different matter and there no error was possible. Unfortunately, however, it happens only too often that people think they have fully understood a new theory and can apply it without more ado from the moment they have mastered its main principles, and even those not always correctly. And I cannot exempt many of the more recent 'Marxists' from this reproach, for the most amazing rubbish has been produced in this quarter, too.—*Letter from Engels to J. Bloch, London, 21–22 September 1890*

INTRODUCTION

THE LINES of the partition of Africa naturally affected the education of the colonized Africans. Students from English-speaking territories went to Britain as a matter of course, just as those from French-speaking territories went to France as a matter of course. In this way, the yearning for formal education, which African students could only satisfy at great cost of effort, will, and sacrifice, was hemmed in within the confines of the colonial system.

Recoiling from this strait-jacketing, a number of us tried to study at centres outside the metropolis of our administering power. That is how America came to appeal to me as a Western country which stood refreshingly untainted by territorial colonialism in Africa. To America I therefore went; how and in what circumstances, I have already related in my autobiography, *Ghana*. I spent almost ten years in the United States of America, studying and working for a living; teaching and carrying out my own private researches.

The evaluation of one's own social circumstance is part of the analysis of facts and events, and this kind of evaluation is, I feel, as good a starting point of the inquiry into the relations between philosophy and society as any other. Philosophy, in understanding human society, calls for an analysis of facts and events, and an attempt to see how they fit into human life, and so how they make up human experience. In this way, philosophy, like history, can come to enrich, indeed to define, the experience of man.

The ten years which I spent in the United States of America represents a crucial period in the development of my philosophical conscience. It was at the Universities of Lincoln and Pennsylvania that this conscience was first awakened. I was introduced to the great philosophical systems of the past to which the Western universities have given their blessing, arranging and classifying them with the delicate care lavished on museum pieces. When once these systems were so handled, it was natural that they should be regarded as monuments of human intellection. And monuments, because they mark achievements at their particular point in history, soon become conservative in the impression which they make on posterity.

I was introduced to Plato, Aristotle, Descartes, Kant, Hegel, Schopenhauer, Nietzsche, Marx and other immortals, to whom I should like to refer as the university philosophers. But these titans were expounded in such a way that a student from a colony could easily find his breast agitated by conflicting attitudes. These attitudes can have effects which spread out over a whole society, should such a student finally pursue a political life.

A colonial student does not by origin belong to the intellectual history in which the university philosophers are such impressive landmarks. The colonial student can be so seduced by these attempts to give a philosophical account of the universe, that he surrenders his whole personality to them. When he does this, he loses sight of the fundamental social fact that he is a colonial subject. In this way, he omits to draw from his education and from the concern displayed by the great philosophers for human problems, anything which he might relate to the very real problem of colonial domination, which, as it happens, conditions the immediate life of every colonized African.

With single-minded devotion, the colonial student meanders through the intricacies of the philosophical systems. And yet these systems did aim at providing a philosophical account of the world in the circumstances and conditions of their time. For even philosophical systems are facts of history. By the time, however, that they come to be accepted in the universities for exposition, they have lost the vital power which they had at their first statement, they have shed their dynamism and polemic reference. This is a result of the academic treatment which they are given. The academic treatment is the result of an attitude to philosophical systems as though there was nothing to them but statements standing in logical relation to one another.

This defective approach to scholarship was suffered by different categories of colonial student. Many of them had been hand-picked and, so to say, carried certificates of worthiness with them. These were considered fit to become enlightened servants of the colonial administration. The process by which this category of student became fit usually started at an early age, for not infrequently they had lost contact early in life with their traditional background. By reason of their lack of contact with their own roots, they became prone to accept some theory of universalism, provided it was expressed in vague, mellifluous terms.

Armed with their universalism, they carried away from their

university courses an attitude entirely at variance with the concrete reality of their people and their struggle. When they came across doctrines of a combative nature, like those of Marxism, they reduced them to arid abstractions, to common-room subtleties. In this way, through the good graces of their colonialist patrons, these students, now competent in the art of forming not a concrete environmental view of social political problems, but an abstract, 'liberal' outlook, began to fulfil the hopes and expectations of their guides and guardians.

A few colonial students gained access to metropolitan universities almost as of right, on account of their social standing. Instead of considering culture as a gift and a pleasure, the intellectual who emerged therefrom now saw it as a personal distinction and privilege. He might have suffered mild persecution at the hands of the colonialists, but hardly ever really in the flesh. From his wobbly pedestal, he indulged in the history and sociology of his country, and thereby managed to preserve some measure of positive involvement with the national processes. It must however be obvious that the degree of national consciousness attained by him was not of such an order as to permit his full grasp of the laws of historical development or of the thorough-going nature of the struggle to be waged, if national independence was to be won.

Finally, there were the vast numbers of ordinary Africans, who, animated by a lively national consciousness, sought knowledge as an instrument of national emancipation and integrity. This is not to say that these Africans overlooked the purely cultural value of their studies. But in order that their cultural acquisition should be valuable, they needed to be capable of appreciating it as free men.

I was one of this number.

CHAPTER I

PHILOSOPHY IN RETROSPECT

THE CRITICAL study of the philosophies of the past should lead to the study of modern theories, for these latter, born of the fire of contemporary struggles, are militant and alive. It is not only the study of philosophy which can become perverted. The study of history too can become warped. The colonized African student, whose roots in his own society are systematically starved of sustenance, is introduced to Greek and Roman history, the cradle history of modern Europe, and he is encouraged to treat this portion of the story of man together with the subsequent history of Europe as the only worthwhile portion. This history is anointed with a universalist flavouring which titillates the palate of certain African intellectuals so agreeably that they become alienated from their own immediate society.

For the third category of colonial student it was especially impossible to read the works of Marx and Engels as desiccated abstract philosophies having no bearing on our colonial situation. During my stay in America the conviction was firmly created in me that a great deal in their thought could assist us in the fight against colonialism. I learnt to see philosophical systems in the context of the social milieu which produced them. I therefore learnt to look for *social contention* in philosophical systems. I am not saying, however, that this is the only way to look at philosophy.

It is of course possible to see the history of philosophy in diverse ways, each way of seeing it being in fact an illumination of the type of problem dealt with in this branch of human thought. It is possible, for instance, to look upon philosophy as a series of abstract systems. When philosophy is so seen, even moral philosophers, with regrettable coyness, say that their preoccupation has nothing to do with life. They say that their concern is not to name moral principles or to improve anybody's character, but narrowly to elucidate the meaning of terms used in ethical discourse, and to determine the status of moral principles and rules, as regards the obligation which they impose upon us.

When philosophy is regarded in the light of a series of abstract systems, it can be said to concern itself with two fundamental questions: first, the question 'what there is'; second, the question how 'what there is' may be explained.

The answer to the first question has a number of aspects. It lays down a minimum number of general ideas under which every item in the world can and must be brought. It does this without naming the items themselves, without furnishing us with an inventory, a roll-call of the items, the objects in the world. It specifies, not particular objects, but the basic types of object. The answer further implies a certain reductionism; for in naming only a few basic types as exhausting all objects in the world, it brings every object directly under one of the basic types.

Let me illustrate my meaning with the following example. Thales, the earliest known Western philosopher, held that every-thing was water. By this, he did not of course mean that everything was drinkable. That everything was directly water or constructible from water alone as raw material is in fact the heart of his epigram. Thales recognized just one basic type of substance.

For another illustration let me use Berkeley, the man according to whose understanding the world consisted of spirits and their ideas. For Berkeley, every item in the world was either itself a spirit or some idea possessed by some spirit. It must be said in mitigation that neither Berkeley nor Thales robbed the world of a single item or object. The world was still full of athletes and grapes, bishops and apples. But, in both cases, minimal basic types were selected, and everything in the world was said to come under them either directly or by an analysis which reduced them to the basic types. That is, for Thales, everything was water or could be reduced to water; for Berkeley, everything was a spirit or idea or was reducible to spirits and ideas.

By appeal to both venerable philosophers, I have sought to

illustrate the character of answers to the first question of philosophy, the question 'what there is'. Thales's answer was water, Berkeley's answer was spirits and their ideas.

In this first answer, philosophers in fact tackle the question of the origin of things. Thales traces this origin to water, Berkeley to spirits and their ideas. In effect, however, they both seek the origins of the varieties of object of the world in something which itself forms part of the world. There thus arises a supervening need to discourse about the possible origins of the cosmic raw material.

It is thus that the requirement to explain the cosmic raw material comes to raise the second question of philosophy. There are two aspects to its answer. In its first aspect, the explanation offers an account of the origin of the cosmic raw material. If, as according to Thales, water was all that God needed when, on the eve of creation, he girded up his loins, then first of all, the answer to the second question offers an account of the origin of the cosmic raw material, in the present case, water.

In its second aspect, it is an account of the extent of the cosmic raw material. It lets us know whether God, addressing himself to the task on the day of creation, can find that there is an economic shortage, that is to say, a shortage of raw material; it lets us know whether an error of costing can come to frustrate God's plan for universe-building.

In the urgency of the second question of philosophy can be detected a certain anxiety about the Principle of Sufficient Reason. According to this principle, everything has an explanation why it is as it is, and not otherwise. Has the cosmic raw material a cause or explanation, or has it not? To deem it not to have one is to enter a plea of exception against the Principle of Sufficient Reason. Now the pressure to withhold a cause from the cosmic raw material – that which is the matrix of the universe, and from which springs everything else which there is or can be – takes its beginning from the fact that whatever cause is proposed for it must be vexed by persistent problems.

According to the hypothesis that what we seek to explain is the *basic* raw material, any proposed cause for it can only itself arise from the *basic* raw material. Therefore, it must either be part of the basic raw material or be a product of it. If it is part of it, then the basic raw material is being said to be a cause of itself. If the cause is a product of the basic raw material, then an effect is being said paradoxically to cause its own cause! A circle of a very vicious kind is thus described. Furthermore, to say that 'what there is' is self-caused is, speaking without bias, to deny that it has a cause at all.

In this, there is as broad a hint as one can desire that the question of the origin of 'what there is' has no affirmative answer. Nor indeed is the vicious circle the only tribulation which awaits an affirmative answer. If a cause is suggested for the cosmic raw material, this neurotic insistence on a cause will open up an infinite regress about the cause of the cause of the cosmic material, and so on.

In sum, then, the denial that 'what there is' has a cause is a claim of an exception to the Principle of Sufficient Reason, or, in tones of moderation, it is a caveat that this principle is only applicable inside the world, and not, from the outside, to the world. It applies only to transformations of the cosmic raw material, only to its products. To apply the law to the cosmic raw material is to fall into the maw of contradiction; even to say that it is its own cause, is to make a merely formal salutation to the principle, for there can be no scientific or significant difference between a thing being self-caused and its being uncaused.

However, it is worthy of note how this second question of philosophy in its first aspect stands *vis-à-vis* theological beliefs. In this aspect, the question relates to the possible origin of the cosmic raw material; it relates, if you like, to its possible excuse from the Principle of Sufficient Reason. If this principle is thought to apply to it, if, that is to say, the cosmic raw material is conceived to have an origin, then one adopts a theist or a deist position. In either case one posits a force transcendent to the cosmic raw material, and which occasions it. One is a theist if one supposes that this transcendent force is nevertheless immanent after some fashion in what there is, continuing to affect it one way or another. If, on the other hand, one holds the force to be strictly transcendental, and excludes it from the world once made, then one is a deist.

If, however, the Principle of Sufficient Reason is thought not to apply to what there is, and the world is thereby denied an outside, then one is an atheist. For this purpose, pantheism is but a kind of atheism. It is atheism using theological language.

In the other aspect of philosophy's second question, the extent of the cosmic raw material is determined. The basic consideration is whether this raw material is finite or infinite. Here the driving interest is that the world should be permanent.

There are various ways in which this driving interest is satisfied. For example, some people say that it is impossible that nothing should exist, that the statement that nothing exists cannot be conceived as true. (And this, by the way, is one case in which the truth of a proposition determines reality, and not vice versa.) In this way, many come to be satisfied that at any given time there must be something. In this way, also, the desire for permanence comes to be more than satisfied. But it cannot be inferred from this non-vacuity of the universe that some given object will always exist. It is therefore impossible to infer the existence of God from the fact that something must always exist.

Other persons, displaying more passion for controversy than for philosophical cogency, say that the world is periodic, that the universe repeats itself *ad infinitum* in cycles of time. But, for this, it is unnecessary that the initial basic raw material should be infinite in extent, for however meagre it may be, it has been infused with the phoenix power of self-regeneration, in its being said to repeat itself.

Unfortunately, the problem of time is a stumbling-block to this cyclic theory. Whatever is multiple can be ordered in a series. It is evident that the cycles of the universe must, by reason of being multiple, admit of order in a series. Accordingly, these cycles can be associated with a linear time-dimension which extends infinitely beyond any one of the cycles themselves. Indeed, this time-dimension must order the cycles themselves, because some of them must come before others. Now it is possible to conceive this time-dimension as itself spanning a universe, in which the alleged cycles, instead of being universes, merely spell out seasonal changes inside a super-universe. When this is done, one starts from a series of universes and strings them together into a super-universe. Thus the cyclic nature of the universe pales away like a bad dream.

Several persons who reject the cyclic theory acclaim the universe as an infinite presence, and seek in this way to make it permanent. But an infinite universe is no more a permanent universe than is a finite one. Even a universe which is infinite may come to an end, irrespective of whether it is infinite in time, in space, or both. A universe which is infinite in time can end in the same way as the negative integers, for it is sufficient that it should have existed infinitely backwards. A universe which has existed infinitely backwards can cease at any time without its infinitude suffering decrease. Its cessation would be comparable to a cut at any point in the series of negative integers. Given any negative integer, there is always an infinity of negative integers which lie behind it. As to a universe which is infinite in space, it can cease to exist at any time without prejudice to its size.

In order that a universe should be permanent, it must have neither *beginning* nor *end*, like the continuity of the negative with the positive integers.

Nearly all who consider the question of the permanence of the world seek to anchor the world in a foundation of a permanent cause which they identify with God. In this way, they hope that the universe will duly be protected. But all postulate something as abiding throughout the extent of time, be it the universe itself, cycles of it, or God. Indeed, the reluctance to conceive time as empty of all content is another manifestation of the desire for permanence. For the historical process is here accepted as an ever-lasting one, in order that time should not be disembowelled. In this way, permanence is secured.

And yet, at first blush, an infinite existence seems to be no less miraculous than a spontaneous, uncaused existence. It is at least clear that the world cannot *come to be known* as infinite or finite. It can only be by the provision of a theoretical conception that it is said to be finite or infinite. If the world is finite, it must be because it is so conceived; if it is infinite, it must be because it is so conceived. The finitude or infinitude of the world is logically incapable of experimental exposure. Nor is it even possible to construct a model of the universe, for any model is itself a constituent of the universe, whereas it is a logical characteristic of any model that it must stand apart from that which it seeks to illumine; it cannot form a part of it.

But especially if the universe is infinite, it is impossible to construct a model of it. The construction of a model implies achievement, a finish. And to start and complete a model of the infinite is of the same order of piquancy as the performance of a man, who, to use Wittgenstein's example, should breathlessly burst into a room panting '. . . minus four, minus three, minus two and minus one: I've done it! I've recited the negative numbers!'

In order that a situation could be coherently described as the causing or the causelessness of the world, it would have to be a situation in which the world could be placed. But any situation can only be a situation which is part of the world. The world can have no outside; and as it can have no outside it can have no cause. There can, therefore, be no *material* grounds on which the adjectives, 'caused', 'uncaused', or 'finite', 'infinite', can be descriptively applied to the universe. No empirical discourse can logically constitute the material ground of any of the epithets. It is only left that they should be postulates.

If, however, one postulates a cause for 'what there is', one is thereby committed to the conception of an 'outside' and an 'inside' of the world. This need not lead to any irreducible contradiction, for whether the world is finite or infinite depends, as suggested earlier, upon the mode of conceiving the world. Hence the opposition is strictly dialectical.

Beyond mere formal dialectics, however, one significance of the cosmic contrast of the 'inside' and 'outside' of the world is that it implies an acknowledgement *that there is* a conversion of a process which commences 'outside' the world into the world and its contents. It is therefore hardly surprising that in the Christian Bible

precisely this is held. There, God is first converted to Adam
through his living breath, and second to Jesus Christ through a
mystic incarnation. Appropriately, therefore, Christianity holds
that we have our being in God in whom we live.

But especially when this conversion is thought to be reversible, a
definite contradiction is created in society, the contradiction
between interests inside the world and interests outside the world.
This kind of contradiction is made articulate in religion; in
Christianity, for example, we are enjoined to lay up treasures in
heaven where moths do not corrupt. We are also assured by St
Augustine that though we are in the world, we are not of it, being
wayfarers.

The contradiction takes effect when with the gaze steadfastly
fixed upon things 'outside' the world, the requirements of earthly
life, which in fact condition the existence of every human being,
suffer neglect. This opposition of interests, this social opposition
between 'inside' and 'outside' is dialectical in nature and can be
used to explain the course of many societies, including African
societies. The course of such societies is determined by a see-saw,
a contest between the inside and the outside, between the terms of
the contradiction described above. It is the recognition of this kind
of contradiction and the use to which it might be put in the exploitation of the workers that impelled Marx to criticize religion as an
instrument of exploitation, because religion was used to divert the
workers' attention from the value which they had created by their
labour to 'outside' concerns.

Many African societies in fact forestalled this kind of perversion.
The dialectical contradiction between 'inside' and 'outside' was
reduced by making the visible world continuous with the invisible
world. For them heaven was not outside the world but inside it.
These African societies did not accept transcendentalism, and may
indeed be regarded as having attempted to synthesize the dialectical
opposites 'outside' and 'inside' by making them continuous, that
is, by abolishing them. In present-day Africa, however, a
recognition of the dialectical contradiction between 'inside' and
'outside' has a great deal to contribute to the process of decoloni-

zation and development, for it helps us to anticipate colonialist and imperialist devices for furthering exploitation by diverting our energies from secular concerns. The recognition of the dialectical opposition is universally necessary. Religion is an instrument of bourgeois social reaction. But its social use is not always confined to colonialists and imperialists. Its success in their hands can exercise a certain fascination on the minds of Africans who begin by being revolutionary, but are bewitched by any passing opportunist chance to use religion to make political gains. Seizing the slightest of these chances, they in fact take two steps backward for the one step forward in order to enjoy a transitory consolidation based on a common religious belief and practice. This idiosyncratic tactic can only create more problems than it promises to solve. For certain, it will check the advancing social consciousness of the people. Besides, in the long run a dialectical opposition between church and state will be re-created through what begins by being a tactical move becoming entrenched. This indiosyncratic tactic *actively* encourages religious forms and pactices, as well as a religious ideology. When the relative political consolidation aimed at is achieved, the tactic is dropped, but the religious revivalism which it has fomented and exploited cannot be so easily checked. It is essential to emphasize in the historical condition of Africa that the state must be secular.

Insistence on the secular nature of the state is not to be interpreted as a political declaration of war on religion, for religion is also a social fact, and must be understood before it can be tackled. To declare a political war on religion is to treat it as an ideal phenomenon, to suppose that it might be wished away, or at the worst scared out of existence. The indispensable starting point is to appreciate the sociological connection between religious belief and practice on the one hand, and poverty on the other. People who are most aggressively religious are the poorer people; for, in accordance with the Marxist analysis, religion is social, and contemporary religious forms and practices have their main root in the social depression of workers. Quick confirmation can be found in Africa, Asia, Latin America and among the people of African descent in America and the Caribbean. Terrifying pauperism, arising from the pre-technical nature of most contemporary societies, combined with the encroachments of world capitalism, a combination which can mete out prostitution, destruction, ruin and death from starvation and exploitation to its victims, quickly reinforces the religious feeling. Fear created the gods, and fear preserves them: fear in bygone ages of wars, pestilences, earthquakes and nature gone berserk, fear of 'acts of God'; fear today of the equally blind forces of backwardness and rapacious capital.

Answers to the question 'what there is' can be said to be idealist or materialist. Inasmuch, however, as an empiricist philosophy can be idealist, even though a materialist philosophy cannot be rationalist, the opposition between idealism and materialism cannot be made identical with the opposition between rationalism and empiricism.

Rationalism is a philosophical breed imbued with certain distinctive characters. In it, an explanation is conceived in such a way that the explanation must create a logical inference to that which is explained. Empiricism, on the other hand, has no such inference to offer. If one kind of event is regularly and invariably followed by another kind, empiricism accepts the first kind of event as explaining the second kind. But rationalism cannot, because this succession of events is not a necessary one; there is no logical inference from the occurrence of one kind of event to the occurrence of another kind of event. Indeed, David Hume is celebrated mainly for establishing the empiricist position, and it is for this reason that rationalists are convinced that Hume was ignorant of the real nature of an explanation.

Rationalism and empiricism also vary over the avenues to knowledge. According to the former, a set of procedures or tasks can constitute a method of obtaining knowledge only if, provided the tasks have been correctly performed, the desired knowledge must infallibly be obtained. Here a fruitful comparison can be made with the method of addition. The method of addition imposes certain tasks upon us. These tasks require that digits be added up from the units column through the tens column to the final column. And if these tasks are correctly performed the correctness of the emergent total is guaranteed. The method of addition is thus seen to fulfil rationalism's specifications for method.

According to empiricism, however, a method need not guarantee its own infallible success. And one finds John Stuart Mill saying that induction, notwithstanding its being a valid method of obtaining truth, is still fallible. For rationalism, a valid but fallible procedure is a logical howler.

Finally, rationalism holds that there are some ideas in the human mind which are innate to it. That is to say, these ideas have not entered the mind from outside, and moreover could not do so. In practice, rationalists do not agree over the precise catalogue of such ideas, though they tend to agree that the idea of God is a shining example. But empiricism cannot countenance innate ideas. For it, all ideas without exception come to the mind from the external world, or are composed exclusively from ideas which come into the mind from the external world through the senses.

As to idealism, it is a species of philosophy in which spiritual factors are recognized as being primary, and matter held to be dependent for its existence on spirit. In Leibniz's idealist philosophy, for the sake of an example, matter is even said to be really unconscious spirit. And in Berkeley's idealist philosophy, though matter is not said to be spirit, but an idea possessed by spirit, its existence and continuance is said to consist in its being possessed by spirit. For Leibniz the world was nothing but spirit; for Berkeley it was nothing but spirits and their knowledge. Since, however, the central tenet of idealism is the withdrawal from matter of an existence independent of spirit, materialism in its opposition to idealism must as a minimum assert the independent existence of matter.

But, now, to the extent that idealism makes the existence of matter dependent on perception, or on the possession of ideas by the mind, I am sure that it can be refuted. Of the normal sources of idealism, two can be discerned. On the one hand, idealism comes of solipsism, whether complete or incipient; on the other, it comes from some theory or other of perception.

In complete solipsism the individual is identified with the universe. The universe comes to consist of the individual and his experience. And when we seek to inquire a little of what this gigantic individual who fills the universe is compounded, we are confronted with diverse degrees of incoherence. In solipsism, the individual starts from a depressing scepticism about the existence of other people and other things. While in the grip of this pessimism, he pleasantly ignores the fact that his own body is part of the external world, that he sees and touches his own body in exactly the same sense that he sees and touches any other body. If other bodies are only portions of the individual's experience, then by the same magic he must disincarnate himself. In this way, the individual's role as the centre of solipsism begins to wobble seriously, he is no longer the peg on which the universe hangs, the hub around which it revolves. Solipsism begins to shed its focal point for the universe. The individual begins to coalesce with his own experience. The individual as a subject, the sufferer and enjoyer of experience, melts away, and we are left with unattached experience.

In incipient solipsism, like that which afflicted Descartes, one encounters a form of argument which is in its essence sincerely fallacious. Descartes says that he can think of himself as being without eyes, or as being without arms, etc. In short, he claims that he can think of himself as having been deprived of any of his physical features which anyone might care to name. Whatever be the truth-value of this, he sets it up as a reason for saying that he can think of himself as being without a body. Though one may not wish to deny that Descartes could indeed have been physically deformed, indeed even hideously deformed, one must, I think, resolutely maintain that disincarnation is not a physical deformity! There still remains a distinction between mere deformity and disincarnation. Descartes' reasoning is of the same level of speciousness as the notion that because one can think of a cow without a tail or horns, etc., one can think of a cow without a body. Thinking of a cow without a body is as different from the thought of a cow without a tail, as thinking of Descartes without a body is different from his thought of himself without arms.

My reason for referring to Cartesianism as incipient solipsism is that Descartes' alleged first principle is the admission of his own existence. On this sole first principle, he proposed, quite unsoberly, to hang the whole universe as well as God. I say that Cartesianism is incipient solipsism because it contains inside itself the seeds of a fully-fledged solipsism. These seeds can be seen to grow in the following way: Descartes proposes to doubt everything which might be known through the senses or through the reason. He sets out to doubt everything which might be known through the senses because the senses sometimes suffer from illusions and delusions, not to mention the fact that anything which is said to form part of waking experience can equally well form part of dream experience. After all, the objects and situations which dreams represent are not qualitatively different from the representation of sense. Since the senses can be affected by illusions and delusions, he proposes to treat them as unreliable witnesses to truth. And as to the reason, though at the best of times he wishes to hold it to be essentially infallible, he points at the well-known paralogisms of his predecessors in philosophy and geometry. If reason could so badly have misled them, it, too, must for the time being be regarded as untrustworthy.

Descartes notes just in time that he who is so anxious about the truth and doubts everything, has been thinking, and must exist if he thinks. Hobbes was misguided when he thought that it was equally open to Descartes to say that because he walked he existed. Descartes, having doubted away his body, could not suppose himself to walk. But even if he doubted that he thought, he would still be thinking, as doubting was a form of thinking. It was necessary for Descartes to single out what he could not coherently doubt in order to peg his existence on it. And that is why he says that he thinks, therefore he exists.

But it is at this point that Descartes runs the gauntlet of a creeping solipsism. Though Descartes is entitled to say: *Cogito: ergo sum* – 'I think: therefore I exist' – he would clearly be understanding too much if he understood from this that some object existed, let alone that Monsieur Descartes existed. All that is indubitable in the first section of Descartes' statement is that there is thinking. The first person is in that statement no more than the subject of a verb, with no more connotation of an object than there is in the anticipatory 'it' of the sentence 'it is raining'. The pronoun in this sentence is a mere subject of a sentence, and does not refer to any object or group of objects which is raining. 'It' in that sentence does not stand for anything. It is a quack pronoun.

And so once again we have unattached experience, thinking without an object which thinks. And as the subject is merely grammatical, it cannot serve as a genuine principle of collection of thoughts which will mark one batch of thoughts as belonging to one person rather than another. The universe thus becomes a plurality of thoughts which are unattached.

It is more normal to found idealism upon some theory of perception. Here, the idealist holds that we only know of the external world through perception; and, if matter be held to be constitutive of the external world, then we only know of matter through perception. Quite gratuitously, the conclusion is drawn that matter owes its existence to perception. Granted that perception is a function of the mind or spirit, matter ends up depending on spirit for its existence.

I am at this stage compelled to emphasize once more that our own bodies are elements in the external world. If, therefore, matter were dependent on knowledge for its existence, so would our own bodies be. In that case, however, perception would require an altogether new conception. For perception only takes place by agency of the senses, and the senses are capacities of the living and organic body. If, therefore, body, being matter, wins its existence from perceptual knowledge, it could not at the same time be the means to that knowledge; it could not itself be the avenue to perception. The idea of perception through physical senses therefore becomes incoherent in idealism. And with this one step, idealism collapses in our hands; indeed, idealism itself stands revealed as the self-devouring cormorant of philosophy.

The eighteenth-century African philosopher from Ghana, Anthony William Amo, who taught in the German Universities of Halle, Jena and Wittenberg, pointed out in his *De Humanae Mentis Apatheia* that idealism was enmeshed in contradictions. The mind, he said, was conceived by idealism as a pure, active, unextended substance. Ideas, the alleged constituents of physical objects, were held to be only in the mind, and to be incapable of existence outside it. Amo's question here was how the ideas, largely those of physical objects, many of which were ideas of extension, could subsist in the mind; since physical objects were actually extended, if they were really ideas, some ideas must be actually extended. And if all ideas must be in the mind, it became hard to resist the conclusion that the mind itself was extended, in order to be a spatial receptacle for its extended ideas. The contradiction is in the denial of the spatial nature of mind and the compulsion to harbour spatial objects in it. For in idealism it is not only our bodies which are in our minds, instead of our minds being in our bodies; the whole universe, to the extent that we can perceive or be aware of it, is neatly tucked away in our minds.

Idealism suffers from what I might call the God-complex; it is what Marx called 'intoxicated speculation'; it is what may be called the ecstasy of intellectualism. The concept of an object, let alone the concept of the same object, cannot be properly formulated in idealism. Having once dismantled the world, idealists are unable to put it together again, and Berkeley has to say that his apple is only a simultaneity of sweetness, roundness, smoothness, etc. It is as if one could not have soup any more, but only its ingredients. The distinction between reality and appearance slips between the spectral fingers of idealism, for in idealism reality becomes merely a persistent appearance. In this way, idealism makes itself incompatible with science.

That matter can exist unperceived, that it has a continuance independent of mind, should really be axiomatic. Idealists themselves hanker after this independent reality when they strive so hard to reconcile their theoretical ebullience with the sobriety of ordinary language. Ordinary language is not just a vocabulary and a grammar. It also comprises a conceptual framework which is largely realist and objectivist. The idealist attempt to reconcile its theory-spinning with ordinary language must therefore be regarded as a deep-seated desire to anchor idealism in a certain measure of objectivity.

Now, materialism is a serious, objective, almost descriptive kind of metaphysics. As a minimum, it affirms the existence of matter independent of knowledge by mind. This minimal conception is obviously grossly inadequate. It is open to a materialist philosophy, but not compulsory, to assert for its second thesis the primary reality of matter. Here, matter would be whatever has mass and is perpetually active; and, in its manifestation, matter would be co-extensive with the universe.

If, however, the sole or primary reality of matter is asserted, one is brought up sharply against certain hard facts, notably those centring around the phenomenon of consciousness and of self-consciousness. If consciousness is to be explained in terms of overt response to stimuli, then it must be distinguished from self-consciousness, and perception from apperception. Of self-consciousness we only have an internal experience. Another hard fact is the distinction between qualities and quantities, while a third is the distinction between energy and matter.

One might unwarily think that the assertion of the sole or even primary reality of matter in the face of the above hard facts betrays an unwarranted intrepidity in face of paradox and categorial absurdity. The key to the solution of the problem, the key to the accommodation of these hard facts, lies in categorial convertibility. But it is not the task of philosophy to trace the details of such categorial conversion; that is one of the tasks of science. Philosophy is only called upon to show the possibility of the conversion. By categorial conversion, I mean such a thing as the emergence of self-consciousness from that which is not self-conscious; such a thing as the emergence of mind from matter, of quality from quantity.

Philosophy can demonstrate the possibility of the conversion in one or other of two ways: either by means of a conceptual analysis or by pointing at a model. As it happens, philosophy is in a position to do both. Philosophy prepares itself for the accommodation of the hard facts by asserting not the crude sole reality of matter, but its primary reality. Other categories must then be shown to be able to arise from matter through process. It is at this point that philosophical materialism becomes dialectical.

Problems of categorial conversion have haunted philosophy at least since early Greek times. The Greek monists, beginning, as far as we know, with Thales, were all confronted with such problems. Thinking that opposites were irreducible to each other, Thales' successor, Anaximander, postulated a neutral monism in his 'Boundless', an amorphous, undifferentiated, undetermined source, capable of begetting opposite properties, the womb of the differentiated world. It seems to me, however, that neutral monism is merely crypto-dualism or crypto-pluralism. For even if they are only in a stifled state, all the elements of dualist and pluralist positions swim in neutral monism.

Today, however, philosophy has little need to resort to crypticisms. Speaking in general terms, I may say that philosophy has fashioned two branches of study which enable it to solve the problem of categorial conversion in a satisfying way. These tools are Logic and Science, both of which owe their origin and early development to the demands of philosphy. The conceptual tools which philosophy has fashioned in Logic, and by means of which it can cope with the formal problems of categorial conversion, are contained in nominalism, constructionism and reductionism. For philosophy's model of categorial conversion, it turns to science. Matter and energy are two distinct, but, as science has shown, not unconnected or irreducible, categories. The inter-reducibility of matter and energy offers a model for categorial conversion. And another model is given in the distinction between physical change and chemical change, for in chemical change physical quantities give rise to emergent qualities.

In nominalism, constructionism and materialist reductionism, one holds some category to be a primary category of reality, and holds other real things to become real only in so far as they are ultimately derived from the primary category of reality. The derivation is such that for every true proposition about an item which falls under a derivative category, there are provided true propositions about items falling under the primary category, such that the former proposition could not be true unless the latter propositions were true; and, further, such that the former proposition could not even make sense unless there were items falling under the primary category.

For an explanatory comparison, one can take the average man. The average man belongs to a category derivative from the category of living men and women. For any true proposition about the average man, there must be true propositions about men and women, such that the propositions about the average man could not be true unless the propositions about men and women were true. Further, propositions about the average man could not even make sense unless there were items falling under the category of men and women. That is, propositions about the average man could not make sense unless there were actual men and women.

In the same way, if one says that matter is the primary category, then spirit must, to the extent that it is recognized as a category, be a derivative category. And in order that propositions about spirit should make sense, there must be matter. Secondly, even when propositions about spirit make sense, in order that they should be true, certain propositions about matter need to be true.

In constructionism, one has a picture how those concepts which are proper to derivative categories might be formed, using as raw materials concepts which are proper to the primary category. In reductionism one sees how concepts proper to a derivative category can be reduced completely to concepts which are proper to a primary category. When a certain reductionism holds matter to be primary, such a reduction has, for its product, concepts which are directly applicable only to matter. In nominalism, only concrete existences are held to be primary and real, all other existences being, as it were, surrogates of concrete existences on a higher logical plane.

Now it would of course be a mistake to seek to infer from the foregoing that according to philosophical dialectical materialism, mind is, say, brain; qualities are quantities; energy is mass. These locutions would commit what are referred to as category mistakes.

Dialectical materialism recognizes differences between mind and brain, between qualities and quantities, between energy and mass. It however gives a special account of the nature of the differences. Both in metaphysics and in theory of knowledge, it does not allow the differences to become fundamental and irreducible.

A sober philosophy cannot ignore categorial differences. But it has the right to give a valid account of these differences in such a way as to reveal them as *façons de parler*. From the standpoint of theory of knowledge, philosophical materialism treats the differences as belonging to logical grammar. This, if one may express an opinion, is the kind of difference also drawn by Frege between concepts and objects, when he said with truth that the concept 'horse' was not a concept but an object. The difference in question is a difference in the role or function of certain terms, and the difference is subject to logical parsing.

Let me illustrate this point in another way. Suppose a man were asked to provide an inventory of objects in a room, and he counted all the legs of tables and chairs, as well as flat tops and backs, then he could not in the same inventory count tables and chairs. True though it is that a table comprises a flat top and legs, there is nevertheless a difference between a table and a flat top and legs. The difference is said to be epistemological, not ontological. That is to say, tables do not exist on the one hand, while on the other, tops and legs exist alongside. In the same way one may admit epistemological differences between mind and brain, quality and quantity, energy and mass, without accepting any metaphysical differences between them, without, in other words, admitting that for mind one needs any more than a brain in a certain condition; for quality any more than a certain disposition of quantity; for energy any more than mass in a certain critical state.

From the standpoint of metaphysics, philosophical materialism accepts mind or conscience only as a derivative of matter. Now, nominalism, constructionism and reductionism indicate that categorial differences are differences of logical grammar and syntax. Such differences are, even so, objective, and neither arbitrary nor ideal. They are founded in the condition of matter and its objective laws. Quality is a surrogate of a quantitative disposition of matter: it can be altered by altering quantitative dispositions of matter.

Mind, according to philosophical materialism, is the result of a critical organization of matter. Nervous organization has to attain a certain minimum of complexity for the display of intelligent activity, or the presence of mind. The presence of mind and the attainment of this critical minimum of organization of matter are one and the same thing. Energy, too, is a critical quantitative process of matter. Heat, for example, is a particular sort of process of atoms. Though none of the above equivalences is a formal equivalence, they are at least material equivalences. That is to say, notwithstanding that the meaning of, say, 'mind', is not 'a critical organization of nervous matter', as the meaning of 'submarine' is 'a ship capable of moving under water', mind is nothing but the upshot of matter with a critical nervous arrangement. The equivalence intended is a material one, not a defining or formal one; that is to say, the propositions about minds, qualities, energy, are reducible without residue to propositions about body, quantity and mass; the former propositions could not make sense unless the latter propositions were sometimes true. As it were, mind, quality, energy are metaphysical adjectives.

I think the matter would be further clarified if philosophical materialism were distinguished from nominalism, constructionism and reductionism. The merit of the latter as a species of metaphysics arises from their demonstration of category reducibility. Their weakness as species of metaphysics rests in their lifelessness. They propose to tell us that x, strictly speaking, is, or really is, or at bottom is, nothing but yz. But they vouchsafe not the slightest hint about the condition under which yz is x.

Indeed, it is only in the philosophy of mathematics, in the generation of critical numbers, that conditions are given for a categorial leap in the generation of numbers.

When materialism becomes dialectical, the world is not regarded as a world of states, but as a world of processes; a world not of things, but of facts. The endurance of the world consists in process; and activity, or process, becomes the life-blood of reality. Constructionism, nominalism, reductionism, all stop at the logical basis of categorial conversion; they ascertain only that conversion is logically possible. But when materialism becomes dialectical, it ensures the material basis of categorial conversion.

Dialectical change in matter is that which serves as ground to the possibility of the evolution of kinds. The evolution of a kind is the loss of a set of old properties and the acquisition of a new set through the dialectical movement of matter. When it is said that an evolved kind arises from, or is reducible to, matter, the concern is with the dialectical source or origin of the evolved kind, not with its formal nature. To say, therefore, that mind, quality or energy arises from, or is reducible to matter, is neither to say that mind has mass, or quality has mass, nor to say that energy has mass. It is to say that given the basic matter of the universe with its objective laws, the universe is forthwith closed in the sense that nothing can become present in the universe if it is not entirely anchored in the initial matter.

Let me suggest a parallel with formal logic. An axiomatic formal system is said to be complete when its axioms suffice for the deduction, by means of admitted rules of inference, of all the propositions belonging to the system. If propositions belonging to the system are made parallel to items of the universe, if the admitted rules of inference are made parallel to the objective laws of matter, and if the initial set of axioms is made parallel to initial matter, then the completeness of the axiom system becomes parallel to the constructibility from matter, according to its objective laws, of all the supervening items of the universe. It is in a sense analogous to that in which an axiomatic formal system is, say, Gödel-complete and therefore closed, that the universe of matter is here said to be closed.

And when a system is said to be Gödel-complete, what is meant is that every non-initial truth in it is derivable from the initial truths alone by use of the rules of derivation. Hence in the analogy, every form or category in the universe which is not directly matter must be derivable from matter alone in accordance with the dialectical laws of the evolution of matter.

I have suggested that dialectic is that which makes the evolution of kinds possible, that, accordingly, which is the ground of the evolution of mind from matter, of quality from quantity, of energy from mass. This kind of emergence, since it depends on a critical organization of matter, truly represents a leap. When a crisis results in an advance, it is its nature to perpetrate a leap. The solution of a crisis always represents a discontinuity. And just as in the foundations of mathematics, critical numbers represent a break in continuity in the evolution of numbers, so in nature does the emergence of quality from quantity represent a break in the continuity of a quantitative process.

It is important that dialectical evolution be not conceived as being linear, continuous and monodirectional. Evolution, so conceived, has no explanation to offer, and, especially, it gives no explanation of the transformation of one kind into another, for it only represents an accumulation of phenomena of the same sort. Linear evolution is incompatible with the evolution of kinds, because the evolution of kinds represents a linear discontinuity. In dialectical evolution, progress is not linear; it is, so to say, from one plane to another. It is through a leap from one plane to another that new kinds are produced and the emergence of mind from matter attained.

The dialectical materialist position on mind must be distinguished from an epiphenomenalist one. For the former, mind is a development from matter; for the latter, it is merely something which accompanies the activity of matter.

It is impossible to conceal the fact that through the ages materialism has been the butt of numerous quips. The most fashionable criticism in antiquity was on the question of purpose and consciousness. It was felt by the critics of materialism that there were certain (usually undisclosed) conceptual difficulties to prevent the emergence of purpose and consciousness from what is without purpose and without consciousness. This kind of objection has been met in the discussion of categorial conversion. A more important objection to materialism is alleged to be provided by the Theory of Relativity. This objection is important because dialectical materialism itself upholds science.

According to this objection, Relativity's merging of space-time constitutes an objection to materialism, whether dialectical or serene. There is a nagging feeling that with the merging of space and time, matter's life in space and its movement in time are snuffed out. But this nagging feeling can be soothed by the reflection that the only independent reality which philosophical materialism allows is matter; and since absolute time and absolute space must be conceived as independent if they are absolute, in a way they are incompatible with philosophical materialism. The abandonment of both would therefore be so far from representing the disgrace of philosophical materialism, that it would be its triumph.

The mechanism of sensation, too, has sometimes been brandished in the face of philosophical materialism. This is in fact a species of scepticism. Sensation, it is said, is our primary avenue to knowledge. Mankind, it is alleged, has no road to knowledge save the highway of sensation. But sensation does not give us any direct knowledge of matter, hence there is no reason to suppose that there is any such thing as matter.

I believe that this adumbrated scepticism turns in upon itself. It is not possible to use the physics of perception to impugn the reality and independence of the external world, for the physics of perception itself presupposes and relies upon the reality and independence of the external world. It is only through some occult reasoning that physics can be used to locate the external world inside our mind.

It is further said that not all the processes in the physiology of perception are physical. It is said, by way of expansion, that if light did not strike the eye, an image form on the retina, etc., we could not see. But the travelling of light and the forming of an image on the retina could not either singly or collectively be the inwardness of that illumination which is seeing. These processes are accounted to be so far from explaining perception that they deepen the mystery.

And yet, to a certain extent, all this must be deemed to be correct. When it is made a basis for idealism, however, then an indulgence in fallacies occurs. We know that in normal physiological and physical conditions, we cannot choose whether to see or not. If spirit or consciousness were completely independent of matter for its arising, there should be the *possibility* of such breakdowns in perception as are not completely explicable in terms of physiology and physics. The doctor, one supposes, would then need to be aided occasionally by the priest, as indeed was supposed to be the case in the Dark Ages of Knowledge.

Our universe is a natural universe. And its basis is matter with its objective laws.

CHAPTER 2

PHILOSOPHY AND SOCIETY

IT IS OBVIOUS from the foregoing skeleton history of philosophy that philosophy could very easily come to be divorced from human life. It becomes so abstract in certain Western universities as to bring its practitioners under the suspicion of being taxidermists of concepts. And yet the early history of philosophy shows it to have had living roots in human life and human society.

Philosophy had its origins in theological speculation. The earliest theological speculations were a conglomeration of thoughts milling around the great ideas of God, Soul, Destiny and Law. At every point, these thoughts enjoyed a practical inspiration. For, in those far-off days, the religious life was one of the cardinal concerns of human existence. That was a time when it was sincerely believed that man's cultivation of the gods at the same time as his crops was one of his major purposes on earth. Religion and worship were preoccupations of day-to-day life, they were the ways in which man conducted himself in his privacy, before others and in the presence of his gods.

Even much later than ancient times, even as recently as the middle ages of Europe, other concerns of life were tyrannically subjected to the religious concern at the insistence of the clergy. Economic concerns, without which the clergy themselves could not have survived, were required by them to be confined within the limits of human sustenance. To transgress these limits was in their eyes to indulge greed, and so to hazard their disfavour in this life and the divine disfavour in the after life.

Suitably, therefore, the chief concern of philosophy continued to be an elucidation of the nature of God, of the human soul, of human freedom and of kindred concepts.

According to this notion of philosophy, when the primary

concerns of human life are differently conceived, philosophy reveals a different bias. And as society becomes differently organized, philosophy is differently conceived. During the European Renaissance, when man became the centre of the universe, the human mind and the ways in which it might fix the limits of what is real became the chief topics of philosophy. There was a growing attempt to identify what could be with what could be known, and this tendency later attained its subtlest and most definitive statement in the critical philosophy of Kant. The rise of rationalism was indeed one whole stream of thought which kept reality firmly within the light of human reason, until in the writings of Leibniz processes came to be mere analogues in nature of logical relations. In this way the limits of the human understanding came to be identified with the limits of nature. This idea survives today in the notion that logically there are no mysteries, that to every question there is an answer, that there is nothing on earth, beneath the waters or in the heavens above, which is in principle unknowable.

Empiricism too was, despite its antagonism to rationalism, a reflection of man's conception of his own position in the scheme of things. It, too, sought to make the limits of what is real coincide with the limits of the human understanding. For it tended to regard what is real exclusively in terms of impressions upon our senses.

During the European Renaissance, when man gained an increased appreciation of his personal and individual dignity and freedom, philosophy responded with disquisitions on the nature of natural rights and connected ideas. Philosophy attempted to provide principles which should inform any political theory, if it is to conform to the Renaissance conception of man. Nor had philosophy in this departed from its early character. At every stage between Thales and modern times, philosophy was firmly geared on to what were, for the time being, conceived as primary concerns of life.

The history of Greek democracy, for example, must really be traced to Thales. Thales spearheaded two revolutions. The first revolution matured in his attempt to explain nature in terms of nature. The second revolution consisted in his belief that the unity of nature consisted not in its being, but in its materiality.

The social milieu in which Thales lived encouraged him to insist on explaining nature in terms of nature. In Ionia, where he lived, political power was becoming entrenched in the hands of a mercantile class which had a vested interest in the development of nautical techniques and techniques of production, for it was on such techniques that their prosperity hinged – more so when their society later became more firmly based on slave labour. The Greeks, as Xenophon confirms in his *Economics*, came to regard mechanical arts with contempt. But in Thales' time, individuals, including philosophers, depended more on their own productivity for sustenance. Indeed, during one particularly good olive harvest, Thales astutely cornered the available olive presses in Miletus and subsequently hired them out at exorbitant rates. Owing to the change in the structure of society whereby social-political hegemony passed into the hands of the mercantile oligarchy, prosperity no longer depended in a crucial way on a propitiation of the gods in connection with agriculture. It depended on commerce with its ancillaries whereby the Ionian products were marketed along and across the Mediterranean.

There was consequently no need to continue to explain the world by reference to the gods. Thales' intellectual predecessors had invoked supernature in order to explain nature. But if the gods were to be explanatory devices for accounting for phenomena, then there was nothing to prevent the most vicious inequalities from arising in society. Where gods are used to account for nature a certain degree of sacerdotal power is inevitable; and where priests have wielded political power, it is not only explanations of natural phenomena which have been bemused with theology; theological explanations for social phenomena have also been encouraged. With the priests securely installed as the only authorized popularizers of the divine will, the only persons fitted by calling and by grace to expound mystic purposes, social inequalities arise to fortify their exclusive role. And since their power is thought of as being rooted in the divine will it becomes hard to contest. It therefore assumes the form of an authoritarianism which, if unhindered, can come to revel in the most extreme oppression. The history of societies in which priests have wielded political power abundantly illustrates this tendency.

In the particular case of Greek societies, however, certain qualifications need to be made. The early Greeks without doubt had a religion. This religion was distinguished by its lack of an established creed. Nevertheless, the Greek priests enjoyed social-political power, by which they could among other things institute action at court on charges of irreligion. This alone was a power which could be translated into political terms even as late as during the trial of Socrates.

The Greek religion was congregational. This fact helped to consolidate priestly power, for when rites are performed communally and not individually (in order that a small farming community should be insured by the gods against drought and famine), the priest is encouraged to come down heavily on individuals who by their irreligion endanger the community or the state. And this was true with the Greeks. It was as their religion became less congregational and more individual that the power of the priest, already implicitly queried by the new philosophies, diminished significantly. The rise of the mercantile class, with its dependence on mechanical arts rather than religious ritual, tended to reduce the social relevance of the priest and encouraged the individualization of Greek religion. It was this growing irrelevance of the priest which Thales emphasized by dispensing with the gods altogether as sources of explanation of natural or social phenomena.

Thales was able peacefully to spearhead this intellectual revolution, which was itself a reflection of a social revolution, because the Greek priesthood did not in the strictest sense form a class. The Greeks, mindful of the massive constricting power which the priesthood could exert if it formed a class, shunned the oriental example, discouraged life-priests, and often fixed the length of time for which one was a priest or priestess. Moreover, the high-priesthood was often invested *ex officio* in the political leader.

The above contrast of Greek society with oriental society should not suggest that Greek society was without theocratic manifestations, as is often thought. Greek society had theocratic manifestations which were intensified under Persian rule.

The pre-Thales hereditary aristocracy comprising the landowning class converted the ancient clan cults into hereditary priesthoods. To these priesthoods was assigned the power of passing and executing sentence *at their discretion*, especially on those who were accused of homicide. As private property grew, so did the incentive to homicide on the part of those who wished to ensure that they inherited property. The power of the aristocratic priesthood was based on the belief that those who committed certain crimes infringed the *sacred* moral order of society, and that they needed to expiate their crimes and be absolved if the whole community was not to be thrown into jeopardy. The idea that the whole community was endangered before the gods as a result of certain malpractices of individuals was not abandoned even by Solon, a contemporary of Anaximander.

Thales' first revolution therefore knocked the bottom out of the theocratic and crypto-theocratic manifestations of Greek society. In destroying the gods as explanatory devices, he neutralized them and undermined the social effectiveness of the aristocratic priesthood.

The second revolution consisted in his contention that the unity of nature consisted not in its being but in its materiality. His choice of one substance for his monism had its root in mercantilism, in the belief that all goods were exchangeable in terms of a common denominator. Water, the common denominator which Thales chose, fittingly reflected the Ionian dependence on its navy for its mercantilism, the growth of the navy being crucial for Ionia's Mediterranean trade.

But the interaction between the alteration of social circumstances and the content of consciousness is not one-sided, for circumstances can be changed by revolution and revolutions are brought about by men, by men who think as men of action and act as men of thought. It is true that revolutionaries are produced by historical circumstances – at the same time, they are not chaff before the wind of change, but have a solid ideological basis.

Revolution has two aspects. Revolution is a revolution against an old order; and it is also a contest *for* a new order. The Marxist emphasis on the determining force of the material circumstances of life is correct. But I would like also to give great emphasis to the determining power of ideology. A revolutionary ideology is not merely negative. It is not a mere conceptual refutation of a dying social order, but a positive creative theory, the guiding light of the emerging social order. This is confirmed by the letter from Engels quoted on the motto page of this book.

Not only is it significant that Thales should have chosen water as the fundamental substance, but the fact that he maintained at all that everything was derived from one and the same substance was of great importance. For, by maintaining this, he was implying the fundamental identity of man as well, man according to him being not half natural, half supernatural, but wholly natural. That is to say, on the social plane, his metaphysical principle amounted to an assertion of the fundamental equality and brotherhood of men. Nevertheless his philosophy only supported a revolution which was in a sense *bourgeois*. The assertion of the fundamental equality and brotherhood of man does not automatically issue in socialism, for it does not amount to the assertion of *social equality*. Indeed, Thales' specification of a form of matter as basic naturally places a *premium* on water, and in the social plane, remains compatible with a class structure. His philosophy therefore only supported a sort of *bourgeois* democratic revolution, and not a socialist one.

On the only recorded opportunity which Thales had of translating his metaphysics into politics, he firmly urged unity on the balkanized Ionian states. This was hardly surprising as he had asserted the unity of nature. The Ionians paid scant heed to him and they were duly undone.

The point which I am anxious to make is not merely that the earliest philosophies carried implications of a political and social nature, and so were warmly connected with the actualities of life; I am suggesting that these philosophies were reflections of social currents, that they arose from social exigencies. Thus, Thales' philosophy needed, if it was to destroy the allegedly heaven-sanctioned aristocratic society, to assert the irrelevance of a pantheon, and this he did in his attempt to bring all explanation of nature within the ambit of nature itself. A revolutionary, as opposed to a reformist, attenuation of clerical influence called not for an amelioration here and there of social inequalities, the smoothing of this sharp corner and the trimming of that eminence, but for a total rejection of the idea of social inequality. That, in metaphysics, which implies this rejection of social inequality is precisely that which is common to all monists, those who assert the unity of nature and of different kinds of things as only different manifestations of the *same* thing.

It was this idea of the unity of nature as well as that of basic equality and justice which required that Thales should generalize those rules of thumb picked up in the marshes of the Nile delta. Rules of thumb allow for a certain measure of arbitrariness and partiality in application. The rules which the Egyptian arpedonapts used in marking out farms were bound to lead to injustices, for they were measured with knotted pieces of cord. Thales' egalitarian perceptions necessary for a mercantile economy, led him to seek general forms of rules. When rules become general, they guarantee an objective impartiality, and impartiality is the outward mark of egalitarianism.

Thales' successor, Anaximander, reasoned however that the unity of nature could not by itself guarantee equality and impartiality. Indeed, Thales himself was bourgeois in his actual political life. In Anaximander's thought, a need was felt for an active social principle which would illuminate and sanction social structure. This he called the principle of justice, a groundwork principle which in Anaximander's system regulated both social organization and the metaphysical generation of things.

In his philosophy, he conceived a stock of neutral material in which nothing was differentiated, a boundless, featureless, eternal expanse whose restlessness separated out the things of this world. These things abide in the world for a time, measured out according to principles of justice. At the end of their time, they give way to other things and flow back whence they came, back into the boundless neutral stock. So whereas at first blush Anaximander seems to have diverged widely from Thales, his master and friend, he in fact only tried to secure similar social objectives by means of conceptual instruments not too different from those of Thales. The early Greek philosophers had a social-moral preoccupation which they expressed in terms of metaphysics. It was this social-moral preoccupation which made them continual sufferers of political persecution.

The point I wish to underline in this respect is that the priests had grounded their power and all manner of social hierarchy in their supernatural account of the world. To destroy sacerdotal power and its associated arbitrary social structure, it was necessary to remove their grounding; it was necessary to give a natural account of the world. In this way, philosophy served as an instrument of social justice.

However revolutionary were the monists, that is to say those who claimed that everything was at bottom the same thing, they were still bogged down once they had claimed the fundamental equality of all. It is possible, admittedly, to regard Anaximander as having had an awareness of this stagnation, for he envisaged not a static and immobile social equality, but a social equality pursued at all times by the active principle of justice. Anaximander was not a lotus-eater. He could not allow society to remain dormant, complacent with the social structure which was current in his time. His principle of justice was one which called for social change, for he could not see an egalitarian society as one in which everything was permanently as it was, in which inequalities remained undisturbed. It fell to Heraclitus to introduce the notion of growth into the con ception of society.

The preceding early Greek philosophers were so bent on destroying the foundations of priestly aristocratic power that they paid little attention to social growth. They were so rapt in their purposes that they also jibbed at the immortality of the soul, Socrates being the first Greek philosopher to make the immortality of the soul a tenet of philosophy as distinct from a belief of religion. According to Heraclitus, too, all things are one. But fire, the fundamental thing, suffers transformations into other things. There is a permanent potential of instability in everything, and it is this instability which makes transformations possible. Objects are only deceptively serene, they are all delicate balances of opposing forces. This opposition of forces is conceived by Heraclitus to be so fundamental that without it everything would pass away. An object is an attunement of opposite tensions and without the tensions there could be no object.

Social laws, too, are conceived by Heraclitus after the same manner. He conceives them as an attunement of tensions, the resultant of opposing tendencies. Without the opposing tendencies, there could be no laws. It can be seen that Heraclitus conceived society as a dynamism, in which out of the strife of opposites there emerges an attunement. Heraclitus makes this strife of opposites indispensable to growth and creation both in nature and in society. And growth or creation is nothing but that attunement or balance which emerges from a strife of opposites. In social terms, this means that society is permanently in revolution, and that revolution is indispensable to social growth and progress. Evolution by revolution is the Heraclitean touchstone of progress.

The idea of the cosmic strife of opposites came to be impressed on Heraclitus by the eruptions which shook Greek society. After the aristocrats had overthrown the monarchies, Greek colonies came to be established on the lip of the Mediterranean basin. With this and the introduction of coinage, the value of landed property as an instrument of economic transactions declined. Trade became more widespread, and the development of a merchant navy to assist the spread of trade further depressed the economic significance of the landed aristocracy. The new merchant force began to seek political prizes from the decadent aristocracy. This fundamental social change initiated by economic drives, coupled with the opposition of local forces to Persian rule in the Asia Minor States, created among the Greeks a society which was comparatively redeemed. Even the thirty tyrants marked a redemption of Greek society. Redemption could not however mean a society languishing in drugged serenity. Internal dissensions persisted on all sides, society was twisted by swift change, but always out of a mêlée there emerged in course of time a discernible pattern.

Strife, and an emergent pattern, a seeming attunement, which served as a resting point until contending forces should once again become pronouncedly factious, this see-saw, this sweltering social environment gave birth in the mind of Heraclitus to the idea that the universe itself is an attunement of forces perpetually in strife. From that moment the idea of a finite history was killed and that of the dialectic of history born.

In the examples chosen I have tried to illustrate the way in which early materialist philosophy of a monist kind is suggested by social phenomena, and in turn inspires social phenomena and policy. I can perhaps illustrate the way in which idealist philosophy serves the same function by citing the philosophy of Anaxagoras. In this philosophy the diverse things of the universe were said to arise from seeds. These seeds of the things that are were conceived after such a fashion that they represented minute universes, each seed in fact containing the whole range of diversity in the macro-cosmic universe. Each specific object was nothing but an accretion of seeds. The whole agglomeration of seeds constituting the universe was said by Anaxagoras to have an external principle of motion. Naturally a principle of motion was required to regulate the quantities of seed involved in each object if this was to be the source of the differences between things; and this principle of motion was for Anaxagoras an intellectualist one. He called it *nous*, reason, mind.

Anaxagoras, too, can be exhibited as supporting an egalitarianism. Indeed, his theory of the unity of nature is in certain respects a more rigorous and close one than that of the monists. He did not affirm a mere identity of basic make-up. He put forward a theory of the participation of any one kind of object in every other kind of object. In his philosophy, nature was more firmly united than in any other philosophy. The distinction between his view and that of the monists, if given social expression, becomes the distinction between socialism and democracy. Whereas in democracy it is sufficient to affirm a mere egalitarianism, in socialism it is necessary to affirm a convertible involvement of each in all. In other words, whereas the monists in social terms sought to transform an oligarchic society into a democratic one, Anaxagoras sought to transform a democratic one into a socialist society.

Indeed, once Anaxagoras had emphasized socialistic responsibility of each for all and all for each, the next step was to emphasize the intrinsic worth of the individual. Thus a social progressive movement, which started with the supervention of a people over a class, ended with the separating out, the cult, of individuals. It was left to the Sophists to achieve this. This phase was given its most definitive utterance in the Protagoran statement that man is the measure of all things. The universe had passed from the hands of the gods into the hands of men. This Protagoran view, which was a passionate testimony to the new place of man in the scheme of things, was quickly perverted by lesser minds into a grasping idealistic subjectivism. In this transformed form, it was a claim that reality was a replica of the subjective will. Indeed, it was in this form that Socrates criticized it. It was necessary to destroy this idealistic subjectivism; first, because it was but a short step from it to solipsism, the view that only oneself exists and other things exist as one's experiences; and, second, because in addition to damaging the possibility of science and the public and objective grounding of truth, it undermined the foundations of society; for it made social reality, too, depend upon the subjective will. The original attempt to redeem society by giving it a united foundation, by asserting the unity and brotherhood of man, now promised to destroy the society which it had set out to save. Egalitarianism desperately needed to be distinguished from anarchism, for anarchism is the political expression of subjective idealism.

Socrates consequently made it his duty to destroy this form of the Protagoran maxim. His social aim in seeking this destruction was to restore the objectivity of society. Socrates, too, was a firm theoretical believer in egalitarianism. He exemplified this in his whole life by his unwavering contempt for pomp, circumstance and humbug. He has left us an undying testimony of his egalitarian beliefs in his use of the slave-boy in the *Meno*: in this Platonic dialogue, Socrates tries to prove the disincarnate existence of the soul and the innateness of certain ideas of mathematics and ethics. In selecting a slave-boy for the purpose of his proof, he showed that he held a belief in the common and equal nature of man. This belief activates Socrates' whole philosophy. He believed in the equal endowment of all with innate ideas, the equal ability of all to lead a good life. Knowledge, he said, was virtue. And knowledge, he further held, was innate, learning being in fact a way of remembering what was already engraved upon the individual soul.

Though in the *Meno*, Socrates put forward a fundamental egalitarianism, it would not be pretended that egalitarianism was to be found among the established facts of life. The reason for this discrepancy between truth and social fact was conceived by him in moral terms. If people were not conceited, mistaking their ignorance for knowledge, and if they reflected, they would all be equally moral, both because virtue is knowledge, and because they would fundamentally all have the same knowledge as suggested in the *Meno*.

It has not been my purpose to argue that all the early precursors of our modern philosophers in trying to modify or support a modification of society conceived this in terms of egalitarianism. But even when they pursued a social line in reaction to the egalitarian line, they were still responding to social urges and social conditions. In a genuine sense, their philosophies were intellectual reflections of contemporary social conditions.

One example of an early philosopher who became reactionary in respect of the egalitarian development was Plato. Socrates' judges and executioners were not half as cruel to him as was his betrayer Plato, also his loving disciple.

Whereas Socrates had affirmed the original equal endowment of men and explained differences between men in terms of education, Plato was no believer in the fundamental equality of man. He held to the original inequality of men which an unrelenting educational system would quickly reveal. He held that some men had a higher reason than others, and though education might up to a point conceal them, these differences were bound to reveal themselves after a certain stage of a thorough-going education. These differences in the level of intelligence, according to Plato, implied a natural division and hierarchy of labour, each man being fitted by nature for functions appropriate to him, the less intelligent being in fact only qualified to undertake menial forms of labour. All political and social power was at the same time to be concentrated in the hands of the intellectuals, in trust. In this way, Plato adumbrated an unconscionable totalitarianism of intellectuals.

Not even this could exhaust Plato's anti-egalitarianism. He looked for ways in which this lop-headed group of intellectuals might harden into a class. He found his solution in some form of eugenics: women and men were to be mated according to his principles of eugenics and thus there would be created a succession, based on *birth*, of people who would in perpetuity hold all power in trust.

It must be said that Plato was profoundly upset by the turn which Athenian democracy had taken. In particular he could not forgive a system which made it possible for his master, Socrates, to be executed. In pursuit of his private vendetta, he elaborated the principles of *The Republic*. In this, however, he seriously betrayed Socrates, for Socrates himself had acknowledged the political system in virtuously refusing to flee from it when accorded the opportunity of doing so. I do not wish, in saying that Plato betrayed Socrates by assailing the Athenian democracy, to suggest that the Athenian democracy was a full democracy. The Greek democracy as a whole, but especially the Athenian, never embraced all resident adults, nor did it aim, even as an ideal, at the redistribution of wealth. Women were not included under the provisions of the democratic constitution. And the aristocrats and merchant class continued to depend for their wealth on slave and other exploited labour. It was indeed due to the availability of slave labour that the free citizenry were not as oppressed as they might have been. The citizenry were expected to remain content with the fact that certain offices of state were filled by lot, and average citizens were able to become judges and executives.

There is one other interesting aspect of Plato's betrayal. Philosophy has its own sociology, and it is not surprising that Plato failed to make a certain appropriate distinction. Faced with one, for him, unpleasant effect of the Greek democracy, he failed to draw a distinction between the theory of democracy and its practice in Athens. Theory and practice are always connected; but not always in the way which Plato thought. While each social system has a supporting ideology, a revolutionary ideology seeks to *introduce* a new social system. It is besides common for practice to fall short of the demands of theory. Democracy could not therefore be made to stand or fall with Athenian society. Plato failed grotesquely to separate a condemnation of the Athenian political practice from a condemnation of democratic theory.

But Plato was himself too much of a reactionary ever to have been content with simply criticizing, even condemning, the Athenian misrepresentation of democracy.

Plato's reactionary philosophy received development at the hands of the Christian intellectuals. For when they needed a philosophy to buttress their division between a heavenly order and an earthly order, it was to Plato and, to a lesser extent, Plotinus, that they turned.

It is important to see clearly the nature of the swing that had thus taken place. I started this sketch of Western philosophical thought from a time in the history of its Greek founders when an aristocratic class, assisted by a priestly oligarchy, held the sum total of social-political power. The earliest philosophers, rebelling against the social order which a theological explanation of natural phenomena encouraged, went to the root of the matter by introducing a different kind of explanation for social and natural phenomena. The social implication of their metaphysics was a certain egalitarianism which theoretically implied democracy and socialism.

As the secular metaphysics with its concern for the fundamental identity of man suffered corruption, it tended towards a subjective idealism, a change which was complete by the time of the Sophists.

And the political image of subjective idealism is anarchism. Socrates and some of his students were largely instrumental in checking the rise of anarchism which the Sophists both by their precept and by their moral neutrality were already fostering. But that very egalitarianism which Socrates was in a limited way endeavouring to save in its objective form, had by his time accommodated elements of the Sophists' teaching. It had bred a rapacious individualism which could not take correction lightly. The system destroyed Socrates. And Socrates' *soi-disant* avenger, Plato, sought in turn to destroy even this limited democracy. In this attempt he only succeeded in adumbrating a philosophy which could be used in supporting a society in which one class sat on the neck of another. It encouraged a new oligarchy. And this new oligarchy of the dark and middle ages, like the one from which we started, sought its sacerdotal ally. So it is that Plato, in trying to avenge the defender of human equality, the man who always said that men did not differ as men, any more than bees differed as bees, helped ironically in instituting his more complete overthrow.

A few centuries later, Platonism having been seized upon, the priesthood set about acquiring an empire and political power. The world was treated to a re-hash of the old familiar arguments, and re-encumbered with a theological explanation of the cosmos; Heraclitus' hypothesis that neither god nor man had made the universe was swamped with earnest pietisms. The priests emphasized their role of experts on matters divine; and, since this world was held to be but a dividend of divine enterprise, they claimed expertise on mundane matters as well. Deeply in league with the aristocrats, they plunged Europe into the Dark Ages and the most terrible feudalism which history records, as the Church exercised her divine right of grab.

The Church, however, was not allowed to hold imperial sway long. Whereas the Pope had been an equal and colleague of Charlemagne, with the accession of Otto I he sank to a junior position. Indeed, he was beholden to Otto for quelling the Italian threats to the Papacy. With the emergence in this way of the secular emperor as the protector of the Pope, the whole question of the relation between Church and State was vigorously broached. And secularists argued that as the Pope had not founded an empire, he could not rule one. Now the Pope's claim to earthly sway had drawn inspiration from St Augustine's *Civitas Dei*, which was itself milked from Plato and Plotinus. While pretending that she was only interested in the higher reality of heaven, the Church was not reluctant to embroil herself in the sordidness of power politics.

With the Pope at bay, the effectiveness of a Platonist philosophy as the ideology of papal sway was seriously compromised, for it could not ensure the continued ascendancy of the Pope. With Plato thus discredited, the Church turned to Aristotle, Plato's telling critic.

Aristotle was a champion of some form of democracy. He connected democracy with knowledge by saying that the truth on any matter had several sides which no single person could encompass in his individual gaze. Any individual could only grasp a portion, and it was through the collaboration of many that the whole truth was attained. One social-political significance of this is the rejection of anarchism – the political extreme of individualism.

Aristotle did not however believe that each man was able to contribute to the truth. In this he was reflecting in his thinking what was a social fact in Greece. To say that each man was able to contribute to the truth would require at the social level that each man should have political rights. To say that each man was *equally* able to contribute to the truth would require that each man should have equal political rights. The facts of Greek society were not in accord with this. The democracy of the Greeks was a democracy which was supported in the main by slave labour. Aristotle criticized neither the inequality of the sexes nor the exploitation of slave labour. He even thought that slavery was right provided the slave was naturally inferior to his master. Such men, he said, were by nature not their own. He enjoined his fellow countrymen not to enslave Greeks but only an inferior race with less spirit.

According to Aristotle, the state is not a mere aggregate of men, but a union of individuals bent on a common goal through co-operative action. It has for its purpose the pursuit of the highest good. Men, he however said, are not the same, and do not perform the same functions in the pursuit of this common goal. At the same time, no man can by his single exertions bring about the highest good. The state is therefore founded upon an interdependence of men pursuing the same ultimate goal.

Aristotle was prevented from fully appreciating egalitarianism by his superstitious reverence for facts. The interdependence of the members of society implies the illegitimacy of the pursuit of sectional interests above the common good, or the achievement of the latter as a mere by-product of the pursuit of the former. He has however been often misunderstood when he stresses that there are differences among men. Egalitarianism cannot mean the absence of difference. It does not require this. It recognizes and accepts differences among men, but allows them to make a difference only at the functional level. Beyond that the differences are not allowed to make a difference, certainly not at the level of the intrinsic worth of the individual.

Thus, it was not enough for Aristotle to recognize that there were slaves. He should have criticized the institution of slavery, for reverence for facts does not mean inebriation with them. It does not mean that they cannot be appraised, criticized and undermined. To say that slavery was a fact was not to bless it. Its economic importance to Greek society should not have hoodwinked Aristotle into thinking it necessary or even acceptable, for if society, according to him, is a complementary and co-operative plurality of men, let it be added that co-operation is free. When Aristotle himself came to consider how co-operation might be made spontaneous, he always underscored the necessity of education, never of tyranny or injustice.

Man, says Aristotle, aims at the good. But how can a continuing slave be said to aim at anything? According to Aristotle, the principle of order in a political society is justice, the bond of men in states. But what justice can slaves be said to enjoy? Aristotle, usually tough-minded, becomes all too delicate when he writes about slavery. At the same time, his writings about slavery have been distorted. When he defines a slave as someone who is by nature not his own but another's, a human being and yet a possession, is he implying that there can be men who by their own nature as men are not their own but others'? A man cannot be discovered to be a slave through an examination of his nature. What Aristotle means is that *if* someone is a slave, then it follows that he is not his own but another's, a human being and yet a possession.

Initial egalitarianism does not pre-determine its own future course. Its course depends on facts of production and the social economic relations consequent on such facts. Initial egalitarianism can be perverted into a cruel and grasping social atomism, a barbaric free-for-all in which each man is said to be for himself, and God for us all. This is the kind of course seminal in Aristotle's egalitarianism.

In order to destroy the Platonic philosophical basis of oligarchy, as I have already mentioned, Aristotle rejected the Platonic hypothesis about the knowledge of truth. To Plato's mind, the truth can only be perceived and appreciated by the highest reasons subjected to the most exacting discipline. Political and social truth was therefore accessible only to the brainwashed minds of his intellectual oligarchy. Aristotle rejected this and made the truth accessible to all and possible of appreciation by all. Plato, to make sure that the truth was really out of the reach of many, deposited it in a heavenly bank. He called his truths 'forms' and he made them the eerie population of a gossamer heaven. Just as Marx stood Hegel's 'idea' on its head, so Aristotle recalled the 'forms' back to earth and restored them to nature, the nature which is open to us all, and with which we are all familiar. He denied that the 'forms' were capable of existence outside natural objects. He held that whoever was capable of observing natural objects was capable of detecting 'forms'. But in any case he impugned the 'forms' on the ground of their utter uselessness as instruments of knowledge or of explanation. No carpenter, he said, first studied a 'form' in order to make his furniture.

With the Church's embracing of neo-Aristotelianism, she saved herself in the nick of time. For she thus adopted a philosophical standpoint which enabled her to make concessions to the Renaissance and man's regained social importance.

Nevertheless, in his anxiety to restore the egalitarian form of society, Aristotle actually tried to arrest the dialectic of thought. He tried to secure this arrest by laying down his categories. According to him, these categories are the most general concepts under which the world can be thought of. There is no object or process in nature which does not, so far as it can be conceived, fall under one or more of the categories, examples of which are quality, quantity, rest, motion, time, place. A great deal of metaphysics in such a view can therefore only consist of the identifying of these categories and the elucidation of them. But in this way also, an attempt is made to fix in advance the form of any future metaphysics. Indeed, prolegomena to future metaphysics are commonplaces of philosophy. These prolegomena are a kind of preface written by philosophers and addressed to all future philosophers. In these prefaces, the authors lay down the limits, the purposes, and the forms which, they claim, must guide all future philosophies. Kant is another example of a philosopher who identified the basic concepts in terms of which alone nature can appear to us and become intelligible.

The motive lying behind prolegomena is a natural one. In certain circumstances, it is even commendable. It is an attempt to make sure that one's philosophical insights shall be conserved, an attempt to persuade the world that all the spade-work of philosophy has been done, that all there is left to do is to build upon this final foundation. It is a claim to perfection.

In the political sphere, Aristotle made a similar claim to perfection. Having analysed the nature of a democratic constitution he said that it was the natural way of organizing a society. To claim that it is natural is to contrast it with other types of constitution which are presumably unnatural or less natural. By a natural constitution, Aristotle meant one which consorted most with the talents of man and the ethics which best suited him. A natural constitution was therefore for him one which gave political expression to the nature of man. In saying, therefore, that a democratic constitution is the natural way of organizing a society, he was claiming perfection for it.

Plato was called to Syracuse to educate a future ruler. There he saw a beautiful opportunity of producing a ruler tailored to his political ideas. He seized the opportunity and failed; so he returned to Athens a disappointed man. Aristotle, too, had responsibility for the education of Alexander, later called the Great. But the democratic seeds which he sowed withered in Alexander's barren ground. These two great philosophers of antiquity, so full of ideas for the 'regeneration' of society, utterly lacked the power to bring them to social fruition.

One interesting point is that, the difference between them notwithstanding, Plato and Aristotle both conceived society in static terms. Their conception was of a society which permitted of no revision. In Plato's view, once a society had been set up according to the provisions outlined in *The Republic*, the perfect society would have been attained. And what is perfect cannot change for the better. In this way, he introduced the idea of a finite social evolution. And Aristotle, to the extent that he regarded the democratic society as the perfect form of society, also operated the idea of a finite social evolution.

Though neither Plato nor Aristotle had the power to bring his ideas to social fruition, Europe threw up men who had the power and the will but not the good fortune to implement the 'perfect society'. Napoleon was such a person. And of the Prussian State, Hegel confessed that it represented the political incarnation of his Absolute idea – the march of God in history. Hitler, too, in our own times, sought to introduce 'the perfect society'! Since 'the perfect society' is conceived in terms of the terminal of social evolution, its procreators have persistently envisaged millennia of unruffled monotony!

I have suggested that the attempt to fix categories, basic general concepts, in terms of which alone the world must appear to us and become intelligible, is an attempt to halt the dialectic of thought, an attempt to freeze it at a certain stage. In the dialectic of thought, a cardinal idea is introduced, and it is worked out in considerable detail. After a certain point, an idea antithetic to it appears on the scene. And, in an attempt to reconcile them, a new idea is produced. And this new idea initiates a similar process. In laying down basic concepts, which cannot admit of revision, Aristotle was attempting to halt the dialectic of thought.

I also suggest that in the social field Aristotle tried to arrest the dialectic of society, for in his treatment of the democratic society as the perfect form of society he was attempting to lay down a terminal to social evolution, and so to thwart dialectic.

And yet his own position represents a stage in the unfolding of social dialectic. The egalitarianism which early Greek philosophy introduced could be formulated in terms of individualism. And Aristotle's democratic ideal with its insistence on an equal individualism was after all a particular way of spelling out that egalitarianism which the earlier Greek philosophers pitted against the sacerdotal-aristocratic oligarchy. To the extent that individualism accepts as axiomatic the initial equal value of the individual, egalitarianism can be formulated in terms of it. But, evidently, individualism alone cannot determine the form of social organization. For individualism may lead to capitalism or it may lead to socialism.

If one takes for the sake of an example the economic doctrines of John Stuart Mill, one must confess that he based them on a passionate individualism. Indeed, so passionate was his defence of individualism that he required governments to exercise the minimum of regulation on citizens. He advocated free economic activity. But true as it is that in Mill's doctrine every citizen had the right to free economic activity, in the context of an already technical society this meant little. In the technical society, this would inevitably breed an economic disproportion, and it would head society straight towards capitalism.

If, however, one considers individualism not as giving to men an equal right to dominate and exploit one another, but as imposing upon us all the duty to support one another and make the happiness of others a condition for the happiness of oneself, then individualism so conceived and practised heads society towards socialism.

It is precisely because individualism does not determine the form of social organization that both the capitalistic and the socialistic traditions in Europe can trace their origins to the earliest Greek philosophers. Indeed, because the cultural history of Europe is the unfolding of a social dialectic, it is hardly surprising that antithetic strands of thought should simultaneously trace their spring and origin to the same cradle. The dialectic would not be full unless the antitheses were present.

At this point I must go back to the Renaissance, because the Renaissance is often conceived of as the emancipation of thought, as the time when thinking freed itself of all social and other limiting shackles.

The Renaissance did indeed free itself from certain *specific* shackles. For example, it was in spirit profoundly non-religious. This particular aspect of it, however, remained largely endemic in the sixteenth century except in the works of a few like Rabelais who in his thought rejected Catholicism as well as Protestantism as huge irrelevances to Christianity. In order to negate the emancipation, Christian theology shiftily modified its position here and accepted a compromise there.

The humanism to which the Renaissance gave rise served as the link between the emancipation of thought from religious shackles and the strengthening of capitalism. For it raised from the economic sphere the unfeeling competition and pursuit of supremacy which characterize capitalism, and transposed them to a philosophical conception in which each man, armed with his natural and inalienable rights, is pitted against every other man. This transposition became a tour de force in the political philosophy of John Locke. It is this political philosophy which largely inspired the American Constitution.

Both the Renaissance and the humanism which it fortified were the second renaissance and humanism. The first renaissance and humanism were represented by Aristotle. He, too, as I have tried to show, represented man as the centre of the universe, and made the limits of knowledge coincide with the limits of the human understanding in reclaiming the 'forms' and putting them back in nature; and also in his fixing of the categories of thought which were at the same time the categories of being. His humanism was a co-operative one, in which each man, perceiving a different aspect of the truth, contributed it to the common whole.

Aristotle saved thought from the mystic vapours with which Plato surrounded it. The second renaissance emancipated thought from the mysticism of the Middle Ages. But whereas Aristotle stood for a co-operative humanism, the second humanism was an atomistic one. This atomistic humanism was assisted by the travels of merchants and adventurers, who returning with tales of diverse social organizations, diverse moral and religious principles and practices, assisted the growth of the thought that there could be no universally valid single religious creed, morality, or social order. This thought confirmed their challenge of the church hegemony.

But just as John Locke's political philosophy was a humanist attempt to assert the personal and independent dignity of man, and make man, not God, the reference point of political organization, so in his empiricist philosophy he attempted to make man the centre and source of knowledge. Since knowledge is thus not a matter of divine revelation but one of human mental activity, man's intellectual independence and dignity was by this token asserted. I have said that in face of the humanism which the Renaissance developed, the Church preserved herself by making a concession here and a compromise there, thus avoiding a head-on collision. The Church became subtle, and, while seeming to endorse the philosophies of humanism, tried to place God at their centre. She ran with the hare and hunted with the hounds.

In the philosophy of Berkeley, empiricism appears to be endorsed, but is in fact strictly speaking denied. For however glibly Berkeley said that material objects were agglomerations of ideas of sense, he told us that it was really God who put the ideas in our mind. Sense was completely otiose in the philosophy of Berkeley.

This was necessarily so because for him our bodies were carried in our mind. The stage could not therefore be set for sensation. So impressive were the insinuations of this Berkeleyan double-speak that the grateful Church rewarded him with a bishopric.

The power of the Church could still be felt, and philosophers like Descartes and Leibniz, inspired by fear of being recognized immediately as undermining the social power of the Church in favour of humanism, prudently suppressed their definitive works which only saw the light of day posthumously. I have already said that humanism branched off into a democratic capitalism and co-operative socialism. The two philosophies of Leibniz and Descartes provide further illustration of the way in which this happened.

Leibniz believed that the universe consisted of an infinite number of units, which he called monads. Each monad was a spirit, but monads enjoyed different levels of consciousness. And matter, in his philosophy, was a collection of spirits which were in a complete state of unconsciousness. He was an idealist. But that was not what constituted his contribution to democratic capitalism. For this, we must turn to his remarks about the nature of monads. According to Leibniz, every monad is completely self-contained, and is completely windowless on every other monad. Every monad is, furthermore, invested with a private law of its development, a law which provides sometimes for the dimness of other monads at a time when a particular monad luxuriates in well-being. And this whole arrangement is sanctified by the principle of Pre-established Harmony. In social terms, this means that every individual has an inalienable right to develop according to his nature, even if his development requires the suffering and sub-ordination of others either in a political or in an economic sense. It is in this way that Leibniz's philosophy contributes to a democratic capitalism.

On the other hand, in the philosophy of Descartes support is given to co-operative socialism. Descartes begins from the position that reason is the same in all, and that *fundamentally* we are *equally* able to perceive and appreciate the *same* truths. We do not have private truths; we all share public objective truths, and pursue them. And even when, because we have not paid full attention to the matter on hand, we have not yet ascertained the truth, we must co-operate with others in supporting the demands of order as conceived by them. Consequently, Descartes says that while he was busy doubting everything in order the better to appreciate what was true, he still conceived it as necessary to co-operate with others in supporting the stability and order of society.

By multiplying examples to show how there is a *social contention*, implicit or explicit, in the thought of the philosophers, the history of philosophy, as I sketched it earlier on, suddenly enjoys a transfusion of blood and springs to life. These philosophies appear *in situ* not as abstract ethereal systems but as intellectual weapons implying social purpose.

It is evident from the foregoing that Cartesian philosophy represented the most radical break in a social sense from the hegemony of the Church and her aristocratic allies. The spread of Cartesianism in the form of free-thinking therefore ensured that there ensued in France competing philosophies which engendered an acute social and ideological conflict. On the one hand there was the oligarchic philosophy of the Church, on the other, the egalitarian philosophy of Descartes with its removal of the region of truth from mystic revelation to mathematical and public demonstration. The acute social and ideological conflict so generated could only be resolved by revolution.

Intellectual tension had been mounting for a hundred years or more. The *libertins*, the French free-thinkers, had suffered persecutions and crisis after crisis. In 1624, the Parliament of Paris, obedient to the Church, restrained certain chemists from disseminating anti-Aristotelian theses. Uncanonical doctrines were proscribed and their *libertin* disseminators were abused as immoralists, tricksters and hypocrites who publicly professed religion but in private undermined it. The Jesuits touched new heights of violence and raillery when they dealt with the *libertins*, who naturally did not turn the other cheek but delivered their ripostes with the full edge of their wit, accusing the schoolmen of forgery, vanity, emptiness and uselessness.

This dichotomy in French thought cleft the nation seriously, and Huet, Foucher and Pascal contributed to this dichotomy, as against Malebranche and Montaigne. By 1789 the divergence had hardened seriously, and only a revolution could re-shuffle French thought and deal it out anew.

In the eighteenth and nineteenth centuries the social contention in philosophy became explicit, especially as law, politics, economics and ethics came to be publicly founded on philosophy. The social contention of philosophy was accepted even as late as the Russian revolution of 1917.

It is therefore not a little amazing that in the twentieth century, Western philosophers should largely disinherit themselves and affect an aristocratic professional unconcern over the social realities of the day. Even the ethical philosophers say that it is not their concern to improve themselves or anybody else. They restrict their calling to disputable elucidations of moral terms which we all know how to use correctly. They say that their professional job begins and ends with the elucidation of the meaning of moral terms and principles, and the source of moral obligation. They never purport to support and maintain any moral principles. In fact some of them sometimes confess their inability to see or admit any difference between the statement of moral principles and brute ejaculation.

On the irrelevance of social irritants and urges to the content of philosophy, Western philosophers are largely agreed. They say that they are not interested in what made a philosopher say the things he says; but only in the reasons which he gives. Philosophy is thus effectively emasculated, and it loses its arresting power. Whereas the great philosophers, the titans, have always been passionately interested in social reality and the welfare of man, many of their twentieth-century descendants in the West serenely settle down to a compilation of a dictionary of sentences as opposed to a dictionary of words; engulfed in their intellectual hermitage, they excuse themselves from philosophical comment on social progress or social oppression, on peace or war. While they thus pursue 'the exact sense of the word', all authority, political or moral, passes ever more firmly into the hands of the politicians.

But however desiccated the new passions of some Western philosophers are, they can admittedly claim to share a continuity with a European cultural history. A non-Western student of philosophy has no excuse, except a paedeutic one, for studying Western philosophy in the same spirit. He lacks even the minimal excuse of belonging to a cultural history in which the philosophies figure. It is my opinion that when we study a philosophy which is not ours, we must see it in the context of the intellectual history to which it belongs, and we must see it in the context of the milieu in which it was born. That way, we can use it in the furtherance of cultural development and in the strengthening of our human society.

CHAPTER 3

SOCIETY AND IDEOLOGY

IN THE LAST chapter, I tried to show, and confirm by test cases, that philosophy always arose from a social milieu, and that a social contention is always present in it either explicitly or implicitly. Social milieu affects the content of philosophy, and the content of philosophy seeks to affect social milieu, either by confirming it or by opposing it. In either case, philosophy implies something of the nature of an ideology. In the case where the philosophy confirms a social milieu, it implies something of the ideology of that society. In the other case in which philosophy opposes a social milieu, it implies something of the ideology of a revolution against that social milieu. Philosophy in its social aspect can therefore be regarded as pointing up an ideology.

On the motto page of my book *Towards Colonial Freedom* I make the following quotation from Mazzini:

> Every true revolution is a programme; and derived from a new, general, positive and organic principle. The first thing necessary is to accept that principle. Its development must then be confined to men who are believers in it, and emancipated from every tie or connection with any principle of an opposite nature.

Here Mazzini asserts the connection between a revolution and an ideology. When the revolution has been successful, the ideology comes to characterize the society. It is the ideology which gives a countenance to the ensuing social milieu. Mazzini further states the principle to be general, positive and organic. The statement, elucidation and theoretical defence of such a principle will collectively form a philosophy. Hence philosophy admits of being an instrument of ideology.

Indeed it can be said that in every society there is to be found an ideology. In every society, there is at least one militant segment which is the dominant segment of that society. In communalistic societies, this segment coincides with the whole. This dominant segment has its fundamental principles, its beliefs about the nature of man, and the type of society which must be created for man. Its fundamental principles help in designing and controlling the type of organization which the dominant segment uses. And the same principles give rise to a network of purposes, which fix what compromises are possible or not possible. One can compromise over programme, but not over principle. Any compromise over principle is the same as an abandonment of it.

In societies where there are competing ideologies, it is still usual for one ideology to be dominant. This dominant ideology is that of the ruling group. Though the ideology is the key to the inward identity of its group, it is in intent solidarist. For an ideology does not seek merely to unite a section of the people; it seeks to unite the whole of the society in which it finds itself. In its effects, it certainly reaches the whole society, when it is dominant. For, besides seeking to establish common attitudes and purposes for the society, the dominant ideology is that which in the light of circumstances decides what forms institutions shall take, and in what channels the common effort is to be directed.

Just as there can be competing ideologies in the same society, so there can be opposing ideologies between different societies. However, while societies with different social systems can coexist, their ideologies cannot. There is such a thing as peaceful coexistence between states with different social systems; but as long as oppressive classes exist, there can be no such thing as peaceful coexistence between opposing ideologies.

Imperialism, which is the highest stage of capitalism, will continue to flourish in different forms as long as conditions permit it. Though its end is certain, it can only come about under pressure of nationalist awakening and an alliance of progressive forces which hasten its end and destroy its conditions of existence. It will end when there are no nations and peoples exploiting others; when there are no vested interests exploiting the earth, its fruits and resources for the benefit of a few against the well-being of the many.

When I say that in every society there is at least one ideology, I do not thereby mean that in every society a fully articulated set of statements is to be found. In fact, it is not ideology alone which can be so pervasive and at the same time largely covert.

In every society, there is to be found a morality; this hardly means that there is an *explicit* set of statements defining the morality. A morality is a network of principles and rules for the guidance and appraisal of conduct. And upon these rules and principles we constantly fall back. It is they which give support to our moral decisions and opinions. Very often we are quite definite about the moral quality of an act, but even when we are so definite, we are not necessarily ready with the reasons for this decision or opinion. It is not to be inferred from any such reticence, however, that there are no such reasons. We share within the same society a body of moral principles and rules garnered from our own experience and that of our forebears. The principles directing these experiences give us skill in forming moral opinions without our having to be articulate about the sources of the judgements.

Another example of a similar phenomenon can be found in Freud. Sigmund Freud believed that nothing was ever forgotten by the individual. He did not through this imply that the individual consciously remembered everything. On the one hand it is because the individual did not consciously remember everything that psychoanalysis was necessary – as a probe into the subconscious and the unconscious: on the other hand, it is because nothing was really forgotten that psychoanalysis is possible at all, for everything is there for it to probe. Thus, according to Freud, all our experiences are stored up, and they affect our overt behaviour even if we have no conscious memory of the experiences themselves.

Just as a morality guides and seeks to connect the actions of millions of persons, so an ideology aims at uniting the actions of millions towards specific and definite goals, notwithstanding that an ideology can be largely implicit. I am aware that in this usage

I depart somewhat from the fashionable one. It is often thought that an ideology has to be a body of writing of one individual, or a small group of individuals, directed only at fundamental change in a society. This is an evident mistake. An ideology, even when it is revolutionary, does not merely express the wish that a present social order should be abolished. It seeks also to defend and maintain the new social order which it introduces. But while it is defending its own social order, it is still an ideology, and the same. That is to say, an ideology can remain an ideology while defending an existing progressive society. Nor can the fact that some particular ideology is not explicit on paper prevent it from being one. What is crucial is not the paper, but the thought.

I have said an ideology seeks to bring a specific order into the total life of its society. To achieve this, it needs to employ a number of instruments. The ideology of a society displays itself in political theory, social theory and moral theory, and uses these as instruments. It establishes a particular range of political, social and moral behaviour, such that unless behaviour of this sort fell within the established range, it would be incompatible with the ideology. What I mean may also be expressed in the following terms. Given the ideology of a society, then some political behaviour would be incompatible with it and some other political behaviour would be compatible with it. Given a socialist ideology, for example, the political dictatorship of capital would be incompatible with it. There is always a definite range within which social-political theory and practice must fall if they are to conform to a socialist ideology. Thus ideology displays itself in moral theory and practice. In the account of some Greek philosophers in the last chapter, I suggested how a humanist ideology held implications for political theory, and illustrated this mainly from Aristotle.

The ideology of a society is total. It embraces the whole life of a people, and manifests itself in their class-structure, history, literature, art, religion. It also acquires a philosophical statement. If an ideology is integrative in intent, that is to say, if it seeks to introduce a certain order which will unite the actions of millions towards specific and definite goals, then its instruments can also be seen as instruments of social control. It is even possible to look upon 'coercion' as a fundamental idea in society. This way of looking at society readily gives rise to the idea of a social contract. According to this idea, man lived, during certain dark ages in the dim past, outside the ambit of society. During those dark ages, man was alleged to have lived a poor, nasty, brutish, short and fearful life. Life, not surprisingly, soon became intolerable. And so the poor men came together, and subtly agreed upon a contract. By means of this contract they waived certain rights of theirs in order to invest a representative with legislative and executive powers of coercion over themselves.

We know that the social contract is quite unhistorical, for unless men already lived in a society, they could have no common language, and a common language is already a social fact, which is incompatible with the social contract. Nevertheless, howsoever it is that societies arose, the notion of a society implies organized obligation.

I have made mention of the way in which ideology requires definite ranges of behaviour. It is difficult, however, to fix the limits of these ranges. Still the impression is not to be formed from this difficulty that the ranges are not definite. They are as definite as territories, even if, on occasion, border uncertainties arise between territories next to each other. Obviously, there are at least two senses of definiteness. The one sense is mathematical. In this sense, a range of conduct is definite if and only if every item of conduct either falls unambiguously inside it or falls unambiguously outside it. In the other sense, a range of conduct is definite if there are items of behaviour unambiguously falling inside it, and items of behaviour unambiguously falling outside it. Any ambiguity that there is must only be at the extremes. It is this possible fluidity at the extremes which makes growth and progress logically possible in human conduct.

Every society stresses its permissible ranges of conduct, and evolves instruments whereby it seeks to obtain conformity to such a range. It evolves these instruments because the unity out of diversity which a society represents is hardly automatic, calling as it does for means whereby unity might be secured, and, when secured, maintained. Though, in a formal sense, these means are means of 'coercion', in intent they are means of cohesion. They become means of cohesion by underlining common values, which themselves generate common interests, and hence common attitudes and common reactions. It is this community, this identity in the range of principles and values, in the range of interests, attitudes, and so of reactions, which lies at the bottom of social order. It is also this community which makes social sanction necessary, which inspires the physical institutions of society, like the police force, and decides the purposes for which they are called into being.

Indeed, when I spoke at the Law Conference at Accra in January 1962, I emphasized that law, with its executive arms, must be inspired at every level by the ideals of its society. Nevertheless, a society has a choice of instruments. By this, I do not merely mean that different societies could have different instruments. I mean that a society can for example decide that all its instruments of 'coercion' and unity shall be centralized. The logical extreme of this is where every permissive right is explicitly backed by an enactment, and where every social disapprobation is made explicit in a prohibitive enactment. This logical extreme of centralization is, needless to say, impossible of attainment. But any society can attempt to approximate to it as much as it desires. A society, however, which approximates too closely to this extreme will engender such an unwieldy bureaucracy that the intention of bureaucracy will be annulled. Of course, ideally the intention of bureaucracy is to achieve impartiality and eschew the arbitrary. But when a society develops an unwieldy bureaucracy it has allowed this fear of the arbitrary to become pathological, and it is itself autocratic.

And yet, a society must count among its instruments of 'coercion' and cohesion, prohibitions and permissions which are made explicit in a statutory way. In many societies, there is in addition a whole gamut of instruments which are at once subtle and insidious. The sermon in the pulpit, the pressures of trade unionism, the opprobrium inflicted by the press, the ridicule of friends, the ostracism of colleagues; the sneer, the snub and countless other devices, these are all non-statutory instruments by means of which societies exert coercion, by means of which they achieve and preserve unity.

'Coercion' could unfortunately be rather painful, but it is signally effective in ensuring that individual behaviour does not become dangerously irresponsible. The individual is not an anarchic unit. He lives in orderly surroundings, and the achieving of these orderly surroundings calls for methods both explicit and subtle.

One of these subtle methods is to be found in the account of history. The history of Africa, as presented by European scholars, has been encumbered with malicious myths. It was even denied that we were a historical people. It was said that whereas other continents had shaped history, and determined its course, Africa had stood still, held down by inertia; that Africa was only propelled into history by the European contact. African history was therefore presented as an extension of European history. Hegel's authority was lent to this a-historical hypothesis concerning Africa, which he himself unhappily helped to promote. And apologists of colonialism lost little time in seizing upon it and writing wildly thereon. In presenting the history of Africa as the history of the collapse of our traditional societies in the presence of the European advent, colonialism and imperialism employed their account of African history and anthropology as an instrument of their oppressive ideology.

Earlier on, such disparaging accounts had been given of African society and culture as to appear to justify slavery, and slavery, posed against these accounts, seemed a positive deliverance of our ancestors. When the slave trade and slavery became illegal, the experts on Africa yielded to the new wind of change, and now began to present African culture and society as being so rudimentary and primitive that colonialism was a duty of Christianity and civilization. Even if we were no longer, on the evidence of the shape of our skulls, regarded as the missing link, unblessed with the arts of good government, material and spiritual progress, we were still regarded as representing the infancy of mankind. Our highly sophisticated culture was said to be simple and paralysed by inertia, and we had to be encumbered with tutelage. And this tutelage, it was thought, could only be implemented if we were first subjugated politically.

The history of a nation is, unfortunately, too easily written as the history of its dominant class. But if the history of a nation, or a people, cannot be found in the history of a class, how much less can the history of a continent be found in what is not even a part of it – Europe. Africa cannot be validly treated merely as the space in which Europe swelled up. If African history is interpreted in terms of the interests of European merchandise and capital, missionaries and administrators, it is no wonder that African nationalism is in the forms it takes regarded as a perversion and neocolonialism as a virtue.

In the new African renaissance, we place great emphasis on the presentation of history. Our history needs to be written as the history of our society, not as the story of European adventures. African society must be treated as enjoying its own integrity; its history must be a mirror of that society, and the European contact must find its place in this history only as an African experience, even if as a crucial one. That is to say, the European contact needs to be assessed and judged from the point of view of the principles animating African society, and from the point of view of the harmony and progress of this society.

When history is presented in this way, it can become not an account of how those African students referred to in the introduction became more europeanized than others; it can become a map of the growing tragedy and the final triumph of our society. In this way, African history can come to guide and direct African action. African history can thus become a pointer at the ideology which should guide and direct African reconstruction.

This connection between an ideological standpoint and the writing of history is a perennial one. A check on the work of the great historians, including Herodotus and Thucydides, quickly exposes their passionate concern with ideology. Their irresistible moral, political and sociological comments are particular manifestations of more general ideological standpoints. Classically, the great historians have been self-appointed public prosecutors, accusing on behalf of the past, admonishing on behalf of the future. Their accusations and admonishings have been set in a rigid framework of presuppositions, both about the nature of the good man and about the nature of the good society, in such a way that these presuppositions serve as intimations of an implicit ideology.

Even Ranke, the great nineteenth-century German historian, who boasted that his aim was not to sit in judgement on the past, but only to show us what really happened, was far from being a mere chronicler of the past. He was, in spite of his claims, an *engagé* historian. The key to the attitude which he strikes in his historical works lies first in his views on the necessity of strife for progress, and second in his ideas on the source of the state and the relation of the individual to the state. Dutifully grinding an axe for His Prussian Majesty, on the first point Ranke holds that it is precisely through one state seeking a hegemony of Europe, and thereby provoking a rivalry, that the civilization of the European state is maintained; on the second point he holds that the state, in being an idea of God, enjoys a spiritual personality, and hence that neither reform nor revolution is exportable, for this would do violence to the personality of the importing state. He also holds that it is only through the state to which an individual belongs that he can develop and preserve his fullness of being. And the ideal of liberty which he is able to propose to Prussian subjects is a spontaneous subjection to the State. Is it surprising that he should have 'explained' Luther's condemnation of the Peasants' War? Ranke, writing history, implements an ideological viewpoint which he at the same time seeks to conceal.

I have mentioned art as another of the subtle instruments of ideology. One can illustrate this in various ways. In the Medieval Age of Europe, when religion was considered to be the main preoccupation of life, all other concerns were subordinated to the religious, and actions tended to win approval to the extent that they supported religion, or at least were not in conflict with it. In the second chapter, I illustrated how economic activity was subordinated to the religious concern. Art, too, became infected by this idea. It accordingly specialized in Biblical illustration and apocalypses of paradise.

Today, in the socialist countries of Europe, where the range of conduct is fixed by socialist principles, that particular art which glorifies the socialist ideology is encouraged at the expense of that art which the supremacy of aristocrats or the bourgeoisie might inspire. The former in general encouraged a bucolic and a classical kind of art, its subjects appropriated from the class of gods and goddesses, and leisurely flute-playing shepherd boys. The bourgeoisie for their part injected a puritan strain into art, and in general directed it along lines of portraiture. Art has not, however, always propagated ideals within an already accepted ideology. It has sometimes thrived in the vanguard of reform or even revolution. Goya, for example, was responsible for significant conscience-stricken and protest painting in which by paint and brush he lambasted the brutalities of the nineteenth-century ruling classes. Here he was not defending an ideology, but was exposing one to attack.

In African art, too, society was often portrayed. It is the moral-philosophical preoccupation in terms of which this portrayal was done which explains its typical power. It is this also which explains the characteristic distortion of form in African art. In the portrayal of force, whether as forces of the world, of generation and death, or the force of destiny, it was essential that it should not be delineated as something assimilated and overcome. And this is the impression which the soft symmetries of lifelike art would have given. It is to avoid this impression of force overcome that African art resorted to distortion of forms.

By treating of such examples, one may illustrate subtle methods of 'coercion' and cohesion. To cope with the teddy-boy problem, many churches in Britain formed clubs. In these clubs they hoped to entice teddy boys by the provision of rock-and-roll music. Once these youths were so trapped, the churches expected so to influence, and so 'coerce' them as to reinstate their behaviour within the range of passable conduct. The churches used a non-subtle instrument which was at the same time not centralized.

In the Soviet Union, too, open and systematic ridicule was resorted to, and when this did not work well enough, teddy boys were moved from one area of the country to another. Through inconveniencing them, Soviet authorities sought by a non-statutory instrument to influence, and so 'coerce', teddy boys in order to bring their activities within the range of passable behaviour.

These instruments all relate to some conception of 'the desirable society'. This is a conception which is nurtured by ideology. As the conception of 'the desirable society' changes, some of its instruments too change, the subtle ones changing in a quiet and discreet way. When this happens, it is said that new ground is broken.

Philosophy, too, is one of the subtle instruments of ideology and social cohesion. Indeed, it affords a theoretical basis for the cohesion. In *The Republic* of Plato, we are confronted with an example in which philosophy is made the theoretical basis of a proposed social order. In that proposal, philosophy would be an instrument of the ideology belonging to the social order proposed by Plato.

Philosophy performs this function in two ways. It performs it as a general theoretical statement to which a specific social-political theory is parallel. I have illustrated this in the discussion of some early Greek philosophers in the second chapter. Philosophy also performs this ideological function when it takes shape as political philosophy or as ethics. Through political philosophy, it lays down certain ideals for our pursuit and fortification, and it becomes an instrument of unity by laying down the same ideals for all the members of a given society.

As ethics, philosophy proposes to throw light upon the nature of moral principles and moral judgements; it also seeks to expose the source of the validity of ethical principles, and so of moral obligation. In ethics, we have an instrument of great fascination which runs parallel to statutory instruments without itself being statutory. Moral laws were never passed; there are no policemen or courts to ensure adherence to them.

There is a certain fascination about morality. When someone asks why he has to take notice of any state law, the intention of the law can be explained to him. If he is not satisfied, it can be pointed out to him that he supported a certain constitution, or at least that a certain constitution is binding upon him, and under that constitution Parliament is empowered to enact laws. If this does not satisfy him, then it can be pointed out to him that the laws of the land are to be taken note of, on pain of unpleasant consequences. But if someone should ask why he has to be moral, a similar kind of answer cannot be made to him. Indeed, this fact led David Hume to say that reason could not tell him why he should not prefer the safety of his little finger to the survival of mankind.

Philosophers, grappling with the question of the source of moral obligation, have attempted different sorts of answer. Many have given their answer in terms of the individual psychology, in terms of the pleasure or the pain which certain courses of action entail for their perpetrators. Here, these philosophers have tried to anchor moral obligation in something, in regard to which the question 'why?' would, they hoped, be impossible. They accordingly expected that the question why one likes pleasant things and dislikes painful ones could not be sensibly asked. If, therefore, moral obligation could be founded on pleasure and pain in such a way that morality raised expectations of pleasure and immorality raised expectations of pain, a final answer would be procured to the question why one should be moral. But this account relates to the individual welfare and not the social.

A few have tried to base moral laws on the nature of the human reason itself. In this way they hoped to give a final answer to the question why one should be moral. If moral laws were purely commands of the reason, to ask why one should be moral would be like asking why one should be consistent. Just as consistency is a requirement of human discourse, so morality would be a requirement of human action.

Yet others, eschewing a psychological or a rationalist answer, explore a sociological one, giving their account in terms of the general welfare or the general consensus. According to the utilitarians, for example, an action is right to the extent that it tends to promote the general welfare, and wrong to the extent that it tends to hinder it. Here they regard as devoid of meaning the question why one ought to seek the general welfare. If this question is devoid of sense, so is the question why one ought to be moral. A consequence of this view is that social welfare officers should be among the most ethical of men.

The need for subtle means of social cohesion lies in the fact that there is a large portion of life which is outside direct central intervention. In order that this portion of life should be filled with order, non-statutory methods are required. These non-statutory methods, by and large, are the subtle means of social cohesion. But different societies lay different emphases on these subtle means even if the range of conformity which they seek is the same. The emphasis which a particular society lays on a given means depends on the experience, social-economic circumstances and the philosophical foundation of that society.

In Africa, this kind of emphasis must take objective account of our present situation at the return of political independence. From this point of view, there are three broad features to be distinguished here. African society has one segment which comprises our traditional way of life; it has a second segment which is filled by the presence of the Islamic tradition in Africa; it has a final segment which represents the infiltration of the Christian tradition and culture of Western Europe into Africa, using colonialism and neo-colonialism as its primary vehicles. These different segments are animated by competing ideologies. But since society implies a certain dynamic unity, there needs to emerge an ideology which, genuinely catering for the needs of all, will take the place of the competing ideologies, and so reflect the dynamic unity of society, and be the guide to society's continual progress.

The traditional face of Africa includes an attitude towards man which can only be described, in its social manifestation, as being socialist. This arises from the fact that man is regarded in Africa as primarily a spiritual being, a being endowed originally with a certain inward dignity, integrity and value. It stands refreshingly opposed to the Christian idea of the original sin and degradation of man.

This idea of the original value of man imposes duties of a socialist kind upon us. Herein lies the theoretical basis of African communalism. This theoretical basis expressed itself on the social level in terms of institutions such as the clan, underlining the initial equality of all and the responsibility of many for one. In this social situation, it was impossible for classes of a Marxian kind to arise. By a Marxian kind of class, I mean one which has a place in a horizontal social stratification. Here classes are related in such a way that there is a disproportion of economic and political power between them. In such a society there exist classes which are crushed, lacerated and ground down by the encumbrance of exploitation. One class sits upon the neck of another.

In the traditional African society, no sectional interest could be regarded as supreme; nor did legislative and executive power aid the interests of any particular group. The welfare of the people was supreme.

But colonialism came and changed all this. First, there were the necessities of the colonial administration to which I referred in the Introduction. For its success, the colonial administration needed a cadre of Africans, who, by being introduced to a certain minimum of European education, became infected with European ideals, which they tacitly accepted as being valid for African societies. Because these African instruments of the colonial administration were seen by all to be closely associated with the new sources of power, they acquired a certain prestige and rank to which they were not entitled by the demands of the harmonious development of their own society.

In addition to them, groups of merchants and traders, lawyers, doctors, politicians and trade unionists emerged, who, armed with skills and levels of affluence which were gratifying to the colonial administration, initiated something parallel to the European middle class. There were also certain feudal-minded elements who became imbued with European ideals either through direct European education or through hobnobbing with the local colonial administration. They gave the impression that they could be relied upon implicitly as repositories of all those staid and conservative virtues indispensable to any exploiter administration. They, as it were, paid the registration fee for membership of a class which was now associated with social power and authority.

Such education as we were all given put before us right from our infancy ideals of the metropolitan countries, ideals which could seldom be seen as representing the scheme, the harmony and progress of African society. The scale and type of economic activity, the idea of the accountability of the individual conscience introduced by the Christian religion, countless other silent influences, these have all made an indelible impression upon African society.

But neither economic nor political subjugation could be considered as being in tune with the traditional African egalitarian view of man and society. Colonialism had in any case to be done away with. The African Hercules has his club poised ready to smite any new head which the colonialist hydra may care to put out.

With true independence regained, however, a new harmony needs to be forged, a harmony that will allow the combined presence of traditional Africa, Islamic Africa and Euro-Christian Africa, so that this presence is in tune with the original humanist principles underlying African society. Our society is not the old society, but a new society enlarged by Islamic and Euro-Christian influences. A new emergent ideology is therefore required, an ideology which can solidify in a philosophical statement, but at the same time an ideology which will not abandon the original humanist principles of Africa.

Such a philosophical statement will be born out of the crisis of the African conscience confronted with the three strands of present African society. Such a philosophical statement I propose to name *philosophical consciencism*, for it will give the theoretical basis for an ideology whose aim shall be to contain the African experience of Islamic and Euro-Christian presence as well as the experience of the traditional African society, and, by gestation, employ them for the harmonious growth and development of that society.

Every society is placed in nature. And it seeks to influence nature, to impose such transformations upon nature, as will develop the environment of the society for its better fulfilment. The changed environment, in bringing about a better fulfilment of the society, thereby alters the society. Society placed in nature is therefore caught in the correlation of transformation with development. This correlation represents the toil of man both as a social being and as an individual. This kind of correlation has achieved expression in various social-political theories. For a social-political theory has a section which determines the way in which social forces are to be deployed in order to increase the transformation of society.

Slavery and feudalism represent social-political theories in which the deployment of forces is not a problematic question. In both slavery and feudalism, workers, the people whose toil transforms nature for the development of society, are dissociated from any say in rule. By a vicious division of labour, one class of citizen toils and another reaps where it has not sown. In the slave society, as in the feudal society, that part of society whose labours transform nature is not the same as the part which is better fulfilled as a result of this transformation. If by their fruits we shall know them, they must first grow the fruits. In slave and feudal society, the fruit-eaters are not the fruit-growers. This is the cardinal factor in exploitation, that the section of a society whose labours transform nature is not the same as the section which is better fulfilled as a result of this transformation.

In every non-socialist society, there can be found two strata which correspond to that of the oppressor and the oppressed, the exploiter and the exploited. In all such societies, the essential relation between the two strata is the same as that between masters and slaves, lords and serfs. In capitalism, which is only a social-political theory in which the important aspects of slavery and feudalism are refined, a stratified society is required for its proper functioning, a society is required in which the working class is oppressed by the ruling class; for, under capitalism, that portion of society whose labours transform nature and produce goods is not the portion of society which enjoys the fruits of this transformation and productivity. Nor is it the whole of society which is so enhanced.

This might indeed be termed a contradiction. It is a social contradiction in so far as it is contrary to genuine principles of social equity and social justice. It is also an economic contradiction in so far as it is contrary to a harmonious and unlimited economic development.

Capitalism is a development by refinement from feudalism, just as feudalism is a development by refinement from slavery. The essence of reform is to combine a continuity of fundamental principle, with a tactical change in the manner of expression of the fundamental principle. Reform is not a change in the thought, but one in its manner of expression, not a change in what is said but one in idiom. In capitalism, feudalism suffers, or rather enjoys reform, and the fundamental principle of feudalism merely strikes new levels of subtlety. In slavery, it is thought that exploitation, the alienation of the fruits of the labour of others, requires a certain degree of political and forcible subjection. In feudalism, it is thought that a lesser degree of the same kind of subjection is adequate to the same purpose. In capitalism, it is thought that a still lesser degree is adequate. In this way, psychological irritants to revolution are appeased, and exploitation finds a new lease of life, until the people should discover the *opposition* between reform and revolution.

In this way, capitalism continues with its characteristic pompous plans for niggardly reforms, while it coerces one section of a society somehow into making itself available to another section, which battens on it. That development which capitalism marks over slavery and feudalism consists as much in the methods by means of which labour is coerced as in the mode of production. Capitalism is but the gentleman's method of slavery.

Indeed, a standard ruse of capitalism today is to imitate some of the proposals of socialism, and turn this imitation to its own use. Running with the hare and hunting with the hounds is much more than a pastime to capitalism; it is the hub of a complete strategy. In socialism, we seek an increase in levels of production in order solely that the people, by whose exertions production is possible, shall raise their standard of living and attain a new consciousness and level of life. Capitalism does this too, but not for the same purpose. Increased productivity under capitalism does indeed lead to a rise in the standard of living; but when the proportion of distribution of value between exploited and exploiter is kept constant, then any increase in levels of production must mean a greater *quantity*, but nor *proportion*, of value accruing to the exploited. Capitalism thus discovers a new way of seeming to implement reform, while really genuinely avoiding it. It creates the welfare state.

Whereas capitalism is a development by refinement from slavery and feudalism, socialism does not contain the fundamental ingredient of capitalism, the principle of exploitation. Socialism stands for the negation of that very principle wherein capitalism has its being, lives, and thrives, that principle which links capitalism with slavery and feudalism.

If one seeks the social-political ancestor of socialism, one must go to communalism. Socialism has characteristics in common with communalism, just as capitalism is linked with feudalism and slavery. In socialism, the principles underlying communalism are given expression in modern circumstances. Thus, whereas communalism in an untechnical society can be *laissez faire*, in a technical society where sophisticated means of production are at hand, if the underlying principles of communalism are not given centralised and correlated expression, class cleavages arise, which are the result of economic disparities, and accompanying political inequalities. Socialism, therefore, can be and is the defence of the principles of communalism in a modern setting. Socialism is a form of social organisation which, guided by the principles underlying communism, adopts procedures and measures made necessary by demographic and technological developments.

These considerations throw great light on the bearing of revolution and reform on socialism. The passage from the ancestral line of slavery via feudalism and capitalism to socialism can only lie through revolution: it cannot lie through reform. For in reform, fundamental principles are held constant and the details of their expression modified. In the words of Marx, it leaves the pillars of the building intact. Indeed, sometimes, reform itself

may be initiated by the necessities of preserving identical fundamental principles. Reform is a tactic of self-preservation.

Revolution is thus an indispensable avenue to socialism, where
the antecedent social-political structure is animated by principles
which are a negation of those of socialism, as in a capitalist structure (and therefore also in a colonialist structure, for a colonialist
structure is essentially ancillary to capitalism). Indeed, I distinguish between two colonialisms, between a domestic one, and
an external one. Capitalism at home is domestic colonialism.

But because the spirit of communalism still exists to some
extent in societies with a communalist past, socialism and communism are not in the strict sense of the word 'revolutionary'
creeds. They may be described as restatements in contemporary
idiom of the principles underlying communalism. On the other
hand, in societies with no history of communalism, the creeds of
socialism and communism are fully revolutionary, and the passage to socialism must be guided by the principles of scientific
socialism.

The nature and cause of the conflict between the ruling class
and the exploited class is influenced by the development of
productive forces, that is, changes in technology; the economic
relations which these forces condition; and the ideologies that
reflect the properties and psychology of the people living in that
society. The basis of a socialist revolution is created when the
class struggle within a given society has resulted in mass consent
and mass desire for positive action to change or transform that
society. It is then that the foundation is laid for the highest form
of political action – when a revolution attains its excellence, and
workers and peasants succeed in overthrowing all other classes.

I have explained how society's desire to transform nature
reflects itself in different social-political theories. I wish now to
suggest how the same desire reflects itself in philosophy. Just as
social-political theories, to the extent that they deploy forces for
the harnessing and development of nature, fall into two lots, so do
philosophies. From this standpoint, the two real social-political
alternatives facing society are either that one section should pro-

duce, and another section batten thereon, or that all sections should produce and all sections should be fulfilled by the value created by labour.

In the same way, there are two real philosophical alternatives. These alternatives coincide with idealism and materialism. In the preceding chapter, I explained how idealism was connected with a tiered society, how through its mode of explaining nature and social phenomena by reference to spirit, idealism favoured a class structure of a horizontal sort, in which one class sat upon the neck of another.

I also explained there how materialism, on the other hand, was connected with a humanist organization, how through its being monistic, and its referring all natural processes to matter and its laws, it inspired an egalitarian organization of society. The unity and fundamental identity of nature suggests the unity and fundamental identity of man in society. Idealism favours an oligarchy, materialism favours an egalitarianism.

Individuals have both idealist and materialist tendencies in them. So have societies both idealist and materialist streaks. But these streaks do not exist in equipoise. They are connected by a conflict in which now one streak predominates, now the other.

By reason of the connection of idealism with an oligarchy and of materialism with an egalitarianism, the opposition of idealism and materialism in the same society is paralleled by the opposition of conservative and progressive forces on the social level. When in the dialectical opposition of capitalism to socialism, the former for a time becomes triumphant, social progress is not thereby altogether arrested, though it is seriously attenuated. But since it is not arrested, it is hardly cause for wonder that the workers of today in many respects enjoy better circumstances of life than even a good many feudal lords of the past. To confess to this degree of progress is not to say, however, that capitalism has been without its shanty towns and slums, its captive workers languishing and finally dying in public squares, victims of hunger, cold and disease.

The question is not whether there has been discernible progress under capitalism, but rather whether what progress is admitted can be said to be adequate. Here we discern one of capitalism's deadly sins. Under this social-political system, man's materialist approach to nature loses its bearings. It sheds its humanist stimulus under the impulse of the profit motive. If happiness is defined in the context of society, then happiness becomes that feeling which an individual derives, from a given economic, political and cultural context, that he is in a position to make good his aspirations. Since capitalist development is unfortunately a process in which a rapacious oligarchy is pitted against an exploited mass, happiness, according to this definition, is denied to many. The achievements of the capitalist oligarchy define new limits of what is attainable by the individual, and thereby push outward the frontiers of legitimate aspirations. But capitalism is a system in which these limiting aspirations are by definition denied to the people, and only reserved for a few.

The evil of capitalism consists in its alienation of the fruit of labour from those who with the toil of their body and the sweat of their brow produce this fruit. This aspect of capitalism makes it irreconcilable with those basic principles which animate the traditional African society. Capitalism is unjust; in our newly independent countries it is not only too complicated to be work-able, it is also alien.

Under socialism, however, the study and mastery of nature has a humanist impulse, and is directed not towards a profiteering accomplishment, but the affording of ever-increasing satisfaction for the material and spiritual needs of the greatest number. Ideas of transformation and development, in so far as they relate to the purposes of society as a whole and not to an oligarch purpose, are properly speaking appropriate to socialism.

On the philosophical level, too, it is materialism, not idealism, that in one form or another will give the firmest conceptual basis to the restitution of Africa's egalitarian and humanist principles. Idealism breeds an oligarchy, and its social implication, as drawn out in my second chapter, is obnoxious to African society. It is materialism, with its monistic and naturalistic account of nature, which will balk arbitrariness, inequality and injustice. How materialism suggests a socialist philosophy I have explained in my second chapter.

In sum, the restitution of Africa's humanist and egalitarian principles of society requires socialism. It is materialism that ensures the only effective transformation of nature, and socialism that derives the highest development from this transformation.

CHAPTER 4

CONSCIENCISM

P RACTICE without thought is blind; thought without practice is empty. The three segments of African society which I specified in the last chapter, the traditional, the Western, and the Islamic, co-exist uneasily; the principles animating them are often in conflict with one another. I have in illustration tried to show how the principles which inform capitalism are in conflict with the socialist egalitarianism of the traditional African society.

What is to be done then? I have stressed that the two other segments, in order to be rightly seen, must be accommodated only as experiences of the traditional African society. If we fail to do this our society will be racked by the most malignant schizophrenia.

Our attitude to the Western and the Islamic experience must be purposeful. It must also be guided by thought, for practice without thought is blind. What is called for as a first step is a body of connected thought which will determine the general nature of our action in unifying the society which we have inherited, this unification to take account, at all times, of the elevated ideals underlying the traditional African society. Social revolution must therefore have, standing firmly behind it, an intellectual revolution, a revolution in which our thinking and philosophy are directed towards the redemption of our society. Our philosophy must find its weapons in the environment and living conditions of the African people. It is from those conditions that the intellectual content of our philosophy must be created. The emancipation of the African continent is the emancipation of man. This requires two aims: first, the restitution of the egalitarianism of human society, and, second, the logistic mobilization of all our resources towards the attainment of that restitution.

The philosophy that must stand behind this social revolution is that which I have once referred to as philosophical consciencism; consciencism is the map in intellectual terms of the disposition of forces which will enable African society to digest the Western and the Islamic and the Euro-Christian elements in Africa, and develop them in such a way that they fit into the African personality. The African personality is itself defined by the cluster of humanist principles which underlie the traditional African society. Philosophical consciencism is that philosophical standpoint which, taking its start from the present content of the African conscience, indicates the way in which progress is forged out of the conflict in that conscience.

Its basis is in materialism. The minimum assertion of materialism is the absolute and independent existence of matter. Matter, however, is also a plenum of forces which are in antithesis to one another. The philosophical point of saying this is that matter is thus endowed with powers of self-motion.

Of course, there are diverse sorts of motion. Philosophers have accepted different kinds of phenomena as illustrating motion. There is the obvious case of change of place. If one object changes its position in relation to objects in a locality, it is said to move. Against this, it might be thought at first that the whole universe could revolve asymmetrically around an object, in which case it could in absolute terms be fancied that the object had not moved. If this happened it would be indistinguishable from the first situation in which the object itself changes its position relative to the rest of the universe; it does not signify a difference. And if these putative two states do not signify a difference, the latter cannot constitute an objection to the former.

The statement that an object moves is a significant one. And when two significant statements fail in the above way to indicate a difference they must signify the same thing. What I am enunciating here is quite other than the Verification Principle. The Verification Principle, as is well known, has two parts. In the first place, it asserts a proposition to be significant only if it is subject to empirical verification; and in the second place, it asserts that the meaning of a significant proposition is yielded by its method of verificatino. The principle which I am on the other hand anxious to defend states no condition for meaningfulness, but only establishes a sufficient condition for identity of meaning. The central idea is as follows: if there are two expressions such that precisely the same consequences follow from the conjunction of the first with any other proposition as follow from the conjunction of the second with the same proposition, then the two expressions are identical in meaning.

It will be seen that this Principle of Identity of Meaning is akin to Leibniz's Principle of Identity of Meaning and to Frege's Principle of Identity of Meaning. I have described one kind of motion which philosophers accept. They also distinguish rotary motion, which Plato illustrated with the movement of a top. There is however a third kind of motion, which consists in alteration of property. If properties can be distinguished from relations, it can be said that there are two broad categories of motion, such that one introduces a change in relation while the other introduces a change in property, seeing that linear as well as rotary motion involves change of relation. If there are these two kinds of motion, one resulting in a change of relation, the other in a change of property, then when it is said that matter has an original power of self-motion, neither kind is necessarily implied, nor are both together.

It is fashionable, in particular among philosophers who eschew dialectics, to say that matter is inert. What this means must be distinguished from what the inertia of matter means in Newton. Newton defined inertia axiomatically as, for example, in his first law of motion. According to this law, a body, except in so far as it is impressed upon by an external force, continues in its state of uniform motion in a straight line. The position of rest is easily accommodated as a limiting case of motion in a straight line. Now it is quite proper, instead of giving a direct definition of an introduced term, to elucidate its meaning by means of axioms. The axioms will in fact set out what one is to gather from the use of the introduced term. In the case of Newton's first law of motion, we see that here too a body's power of linear self-motion is denied.

Indeed, Newton would also deny a body's power of rotary self-motion. To borrow a word invented by Whitehead, the inertia of matter corresponds to its pushiness.

When it is enquired what the philosophers mean by the inertness of matter, something different transpires. In reality the philosophers seek an intellectual parallel to physical motion, and deny this of matter. Hence, we find them harping incontinently on the 'stupidity' of matter. They mean by this that matter is incapable of intellectual action, neither thinking, perceiving nor feeling. Of course, they are grateful for Newton's denial of the physical activity of matter. They take this up and increase it with a further denial of the intellectual activity of matter. Hence, when a philosopher says that matter is 'stupid', he does not mean that it is slow-witted, but that it has no wit at all. In this denial of activity, both physical and mental, of matter, it is however not unusual for philosophers to contradict themselves. If one looks through Locke's magnum opus, *The Essay on Human Understanding*, one quickly comes upon such contradictions.

There Locke denies that matter is active, attributing all activity to spirit. Nevertheless, in his theory of perception, he says that corpuscles *travel* from a *perceived object* to our appropriate organ of sense in order that we should be able to perceive it. These corpuscles are said by him to be parts of the perceived object which detach themselves and subject us to a kind of radiative bombardment. Here, Locke patently contradicts himself. For this activity of matter is not said by him to be induced, but original, natural.

But even the theory of gravity, while it does explain the current motion of bodies (including rest), is properly silent over the question of antecedents. It does not face the question why bodies move at all, how it is that the heavenly bodies, for example, come to be moving, but only how they keep moving and why they keep moving as they do.

And yet, all those who conceive the universe in terms of an original super-atom which multiplied internal stresses to such a pitch as to burst asunder, thereby imply that matter has powers of self-motion, for they do not conceive this primordial building-up of internal stresses in terms of *externally* impressed forces.

Both the phenomenon of radiation and the wave mechanics of quantum theory indubitably presuppose that body has original powers of self-motion even in that sense which requires something other than change of property. If matter perpetrates a spontaneous emission, then to the extent that there is an emission of particles there is motion; to the extent that this emission is spontaneous, there is self-motion.

The classical philosophers have in fact been over-impressed by at least two considerations. The first is that we do not discern a direct phenomenon of radiation or corpuscular motion by any of our celebrated five senses. But we do see apples thrown to go up. And we observe feathers blown to make them air-borne. By contrast, even though we know of cases where humans and animals are pushed, we witness day after day the more overt and directly obtrusive phenomenon of spontaneous motion in living things. Our classical philosophers have then without much ado closed the dossier, pleasantly identifying the limits of their own knowledge with the limits of what can be.

Now, if one wishes to maintain the philosophical inertness of matter, one must ascribe the phenomenal self-motion of bodies to some non-material principle, usually a soul or a spirit. This soul or spirit may of course be said to inhere in matter or to be external to it. But even when it is said that there is a spirit or a soul in matter which is responsible for its spontaneous motion, it will not have been said that in *every* case of phenomenal spontaneous motion of a body there must be presumed a spirit concealed in the body, a ghost lurking in the machine. Hence the philosophical inertness of matter is not achieved by the mere postulate of spirit or soul. It is in fact made a defining characteristic of matter that it is philosophically inert.

In the postulate of a soul or spirit, vitalism and diverse forms of occultism could easily be provided sustenance and defence. But in this also, we find the second consideration which has over-impressed philosophers. This is the idea of intention. It was thought that spontaneous motion could only be deliberate or purposeful, subsuming the idea of intention in any case. Deliberateness, purpose, intention was at the same time exclusively attributed only to living things, and not even to all living things at that. Matter, in itself non-living, was therefore held to be incapable of deliberateness, purpose or intention. Spontaneity of any sort could not therefore be ascribed to it. This is in fact at the heart of philosophical inertness which is quaintly called 'stupidity'!

In a way, it is not the philosophers of today but the natural scientists who are the successors of the ancient philosophers. Attentive to the phenomenon of radiation, that of spontaneous emission of particles of matter, and Newton's silence over the source of the original motion of bodies, one can, if an 'inert' philosopher, embrace a thorough-going animism, and infuse non-living matter with a plethora of spirits, or one can correctly abandon the now groundless denial of the capacity of matter for self-motion.

Indeed, the philosophical ancestor of all Western philosophers, Thales, was stared in the face by both alternatives. He had said that the world was not to be explained in terms of super-nature, and had accordingly said that everything was water. It now fell upon him to explain why hosts of things were not 'watery'. The minimum he could do was to put a principle of change in water itself, so that by the operation of that principle, a transmutation from the state we know as water to other things would be possible. But if he was not to abandon his first statement that everything is water, the principle must permit only geometrical changes in water, that is, in its operation, it must be limited to the rarefaction and condensation of water. For this, the principle needed to be a principle of motion. Hence, he said that things were full of gods. Though this smells unpleasantly of animism, he only meant, through asserting the capacity of matter for spontaneous self-motion, to reject its inertness. In saying things were full of gods, he did not mean that every object was the locus of some god, for his whole philosophical revolution consisted in his neutralizing of the gods, his rendering them irrelevant for purposes of explanation of the objects and processes of the world. It is his idiom, not his thought, which was picturesque. Just as Aristotle was later to recover the forms from Plato's heaven and restore them to matter, so Thales was now retrieving the source of motion and the cause of processes from the priests' heaven for matter.

Matter is not inert in the sense of the philosophers. It is capable of self-motion both in the sense of change of relation, and in the sense of change of property. But matter has inertia. Inertia and inertness have been sufficiently distinguished, and while inertness implies inertia, inertia does not imply inertness.

The initial assertions of what I put forward as philosophical consciencism are therefore twofold. First, there is the assertion of the absolute and independent existence of matter; second, there is the assertion of the capacity of matter for spontaneous self-motion. To the extent of these two initial assertions, philosophical consciencism is deeply materialist.

There is a supreme need to distinguish here between the materialism which is involved in philosophical consciencism and that materialism which implies the sole existence of matter. I pointed out in the first chapter that a materialist philosophy which accepts the primary reality of matter must either deny other categories of being, or else claim that they are one and all reducible without left-overs to matter. If this does not present a dilemma, at least the choice is often painful. In a materialist philosophy admitting the primary reality of matter, if spirit is accepted as a category of being, non-residual reduction to matter must be claimed. Furthermore, the phenomenon of consciousness, like that of self-consciousness, must be held to be in the ultimate analysis nothing but an aspect of matter.

Strictly speaking, the assertion of the sole reality of matter is atheistic, for pantheism, too, is a species of atheism. Philosophical consciencism, even though deeply rooted in materialism, is not necessarily atheistic.

According to philosophical consciencism, certain activities possessing all the syndromes of purpose may still be the direct activity of matter. Such activity is widespread and is characterized by a non-apperceptive response to stimulus; that is to say, it is characterized by a response to stimulus emptied of all self-aware-ness, a response devoid of any cognition beyond the reaction to that which is for the time being acting as stimulus. Instinctive response is this kind of activity, for in instinctive response there is a non-apperceptive response to stimulus, a response which is not con-ditioned by any realization of a possible relation of purpose between the stimulus and the stimulated. On the other hand, apperceptive response is deliberate. Here, there is a self-awareness and an appraisal of the situation involving stimulus and response.

The suspicion that living things exhibit non-apperceptive response is not new. Indeed, Descartes thought that the response of all non-human animals was non-apperceptive. He therefore denied that non-human animals possessed souls, remaining content to believe that all the actions of such animals could be given a mechanical explanation which is complete. But even humans are not entirely above non-apperceptive response. Indeed a response that starts by being apperceptive could in time be rendered non-apperceptive by the technique of producing a conditioned reflex.

Aristotle had, before Descartes, maintained a similar opinion, that only humans were capable of a self-conscious, apperceptive response. This opinion of Aristotle's was confirmed in his invention of the vegetable and the animal souls, as distinct from the rational soul.

It might seem that a philosophical position which accepts a duality of the Cartesian type cannot comfortably treat all the actions of animals as purely mechanical. For this kind of duality, there should ensue a nagging doubt, the doubt whether spirit as a category should not really be excised with Occam's razor. Accord-ing to Occam's razor, entities should not be multiplied without logical need.

But according to Cartesian duality, there are two irreducible types of substance. There is spiritual substance which is purely active, thinks and is non-extended. Then there is matter which is purely extended and is inert in the philosopher's sense. Now a great many of the actions of animals are, as outward marks, quite similar to those of men. It is therefore a kind of special pleading to hold that these actions are spirit-produced in the one case and not in the other, especially since Descartes makes an issue of the existence of minds other than his own and God's.

In order to remove this feeling that Occam's razor might be applied to shave off spirit, it is necessary to show, as distinct from claiming, that actions which have syndromes of being mind-inspired can result from mere matter. To do this is to show how some mind-language is reducible without residue to body-language. That is, to show how expressions which might be used in describing spirit-directed operations can be shown to be completely apt in describing mechanical action; almost to show, indeed, that rudimentary minds are nothing but active matter. That this is so was in fact explicitly claimed by Leibniz, who said that matter was rudimentary mind, thereby breaking the categorial ice between matter and mind.

In the first chapter, I discussed at some length how categorial conversion or reduction is possible, making free reference in the course of the discussion to the work of logicians. If spiritual phenomena are in fact the outcome of material phenomena, then it is hardly surprising that environment, which is but a disposition of matter, can enhance, intensify, even develop the consciousness. Furthermore, the mind-body problem is solved. This solution of the mind-body problem has sometimes taken the form of cutting the Gordian knot. The mind-body problem arises in the following manner. If one says that there are only two types of substances, matter and mind, and furthermore allows interaction between them, then the question arises how there can be interaction between substances which are so disparate. Mind is purely active, thinks, and is unextended; matter is passive, extended and is without awareness. If one asserts the sole reality of matter, as extreme materialists do, or if one asserts the sole reality of spirit as Leibniz must be deemed to have done, then the mind-body problem is solved by removing the conditions in which the perplexity arises. This is to cut the Gordian knot, for now mind and body will not be disparate, but will either both be forms of matter or both be forms of spirit.

In philosophical consciencism, however, the interaction of mind and body is accepted as a fact. The philosophical perplexity which darkens this interaction is removed by the demonstration of the possibility of categorial conversion. Categorial conversion must be distinguished from parallelism. Descartes himself tried to solve the mind-body problem by resorting to a kind of parallelism. He instituted parallel occurrences, and thus explained pain as that grief which the soul felt at the damage to its body. On this point, as on several others, Descartes was assailed by the critical acumen of the Ghanian philosopher Anthony William Amo. According to Amo, all that the soul could do on Descartes' terms is to take cognizance of the fact that there is a hole in its body or a contusion on it, and unless knowledge is itself painful, the mind could not be said to grieve thereat. Of course, if the mind could be said to grieve in this way, on bare knowledge of the state of the body, then one *might* say that the body could affect the mind. But not so necessarily, for, strictly speaking, according to Descartes the body does not affect the mind, but the mind *commiserates* with the body.

Philosophical consciencism has no room for a mere parallelism on the mind-body problem. For philosophical consciencism *retains* the two categories of mind and body, *recognizes* the problem by accepting the fact of interaction, but offers a solution thereto. Parallelism, while recognizing the two categories, in fact denies interaction. The solution offered by philosophical consciencism is by way of categorial conversion.

According to philosophical consciencism, qualities are generated by matter. Behind any qualitative appearance, there stands a quantitative disposition of matter, such that the qualitative appearance is a surrogate of the quantitative disposition. I do not mean by this that qualities are the quantities themselves. I am not, for example, saying that a colour is the same thing as a certain wavelength. Of course the wave-length is not the colour, though we do know, thanks to the physicists, that individual colours are tied to characteristic wave-lengths. What I am however saying is that the colour is precisely the visual surrogate of a wave-length. A colour is the eye's mode of impression of a wave with certain mathematical properties; it is the visual surrogate of a quantitative disposition of matter. Sounds, similarly, are the ear's mode of impression of waves with certain properties. In general, sensations and perceptions are sensory surrogates of quantitative dispositions of matter. All natural properties, whatever property is discernible by medium of one sense or more, are nothing but sensory surrogates of quantitative dispositions of matter.

In the first chapter, I refuted the claim that Einstein's Theory of Relativity was incompatible with materialism. The gravamen of the objection was that philosophical materialism requires the absolute and independent existence of space and time as necessary receptacles for matter. At that point, I explained that there was no conflict with the Theory of Relativity, and also that materialism was itself inconsistent with the absolute and independent existence of space or time.

If the sole existence of matter is asserted, then space and time, in so far as they are not matter, must be unreal. Philosophical consciencism does not assert the sole reality of matter. Rather it asserts the primary reality of matter. Here again, if space were absolute and independent, matter could not with respect to it be primary. Therefore philosophical consciencism, in asserting the primary existence of matter, also maintains that space must, to the extent that it is real, derive its properties from those of matter through a categorial conversion. And since the properties of space are geometrical, it then follows from philosophical consciencism that the geometry of space is determined by the properties of matter.

When one now turns to Einstein's General Theory of Relativity, one finds exactly the same conclusion there. For in his Theory, Einstein relies on a principle of Mach's about the conditions of significance to affirm that the properties of space are fixed by the masses of bodies in a gravitational field. This principle of Einstein's, like philosophical consciencism, rejects the absolute and independent existence of space. With regard to space, relativity and philosophical consciencism are mutually consistent.

In discussing the possibility of categorial conversion, I said that two approaches were available to philosophy. First, the possibility of categorial conversion could be demonstrated in conceptual terms. This has been achieved by modern logic. Second, models fulfilling the conditions of categorial conversion might be cited. Such models are offered by modern science.

Philosophical consciencism claims the reality of categorial conversion. But if the conversion from one category to another category is not to represent a mere apparition, a philosophical will-o'-the-wisp, then such a conversion must represent a variation in the mass of its initial matter. The conversion is produced by a dialectical process, and if it is from a lower logical type to a higher logical type, it involves loss of mass.

Here again, that loss of mass actually takes place is deducible from Einstein's General Theory of Relativity. It follows from this Theory that every chemical change from simpler substances to more complex substances, in so far as it entails the emergence of new properties, represents a loss of mass. Indeed, it represents a conversion of part of the mass of matter. In Einstein's Theory, the loss is calculable according to the general formula $e = mc^2$ where e represents ergs of energy, m mass, and c the velocity of light. If, for example, one gram of mass were substituted for m, the equivalence in ergs of energy will be 9×20^{10} ergs, for in this case e will be equal to c^2. According to philosophical consciencism, however, though the whole of this amount of mass is converted, it is not all of it which is converted to the emergent properties. In actual chemical changes, some of it transpires as heat.

It is this reality of categorial conversion which prompts philosophical consciencism to assert not the sole reality of matter, but its primary reality. If higher categories are only surrogates of quantitative processes of matter, they are still not empty apparitions, but are quite real.

It follows from this that in philosophical consciencism, matter is capable of dialectic change, for if natural properties are nothing but surrogates of quantitative dispositions of matter, then since natural properties change, matter must change in quantitative disposition. And matter, in being a plenum of forces in *tension*, already contains the incipient change in disposition which is necessary to bring about a change in quality or property. Force itself is the way in which particles of matter exist; it is their mathematical or quantitative constitution. Force is not a description of a particle of matter; it is not something which particles of matter wear on their face. Rather, it is internal to them.

Since matter is a plenum of forces in tension, and since tension implies incipient change, matter must have the power of self-motion original to it. Without self-motion, dialectical change would be impossible.

By a dialectical change, I mean the emergence of a third factor of a higher logical type from the tension between two factors or two sets of factors of a lower logical type. Matter belongs to one logical type, properties and qualities of matter to a higher logical type, properties of properties to an even higher logical type.

This appropriately raises questions of an epistemological nature about consciencism. Epistemological problems are those which concern the nature of knowledge, and its types, and also the avenues to them which are open to the mind. Consciencism, by avoiding the assertion of the sole reality of matter, prepares itself for the painless recognition of the objectivity of different types of being. Indeed, the conception of dialectic is itself connected with a recognition of different types of being. Types of being are logical types. If they form a scale of being, it is not to be inferred that this scale is correlated with a scale of value. The types are logical types, such that material objects form one logical type; those general terms, which can be applied in description only to material objects, form a higher logical type; those general terms which can be applied in description to general terms of the first group form another logical type which is even higher.

Material objects and their properties belong to different logical types, and so do material objects and mind. It is these differences in type which make categorial absurdity possible. By a categorial absurdity, I mean that special absurdity which arises from coupling types of terms which should not be coupled. Terms can be coupled only when they belong to the same type or belong to proximate types. Thus 'people' and 'independence' belong to proximate types, and may therefore be coupled as in the proposition 'we are an independent people'. But the number two and 'red' neither belong to the same type nor belong to proximate types; hence, not unexpectedly, the proposition 'the number two is red', which couples them, does commit a categorial absurdity.

In the same way, terms which can be coupled with philosophical surrogates in description of the latter cannot be coupled with the items which give rise to the surrogates, though there is nothing which is incapable of translation, without residue, to propositions about these items whose surrogates they are.

Terms which can be coupled with philosophical surrogates in description of them cannot be coupled with the items which give rise to the surrogates, because if a term can be coupled with a philosophical surrogate, it must be of the same logical type as the philosophical surrogate, or, if it is in description of it, must be of a type higher than and proximate to that to which the surrogate belongs. Terms which can be coupled in description with a philosophical surrogate must be one logical type higher than the surrogate, since such terms are always one type higher than their subjects. As such these terms are at least two types higher than the items which give rise to the surrogate. They cannot therefore be ascribed even by way of complement. One cannot say that the number two is a red thing (complement) any more than one can say that the number two is red (description).

This epistemological consequence of philosophical consciencism provides an antecedent philosophical justification for such pursuits as the investigation of the nature of mind by the exclusive means of the investigation of the nature and functioning of brain. This is a great advantage, for as the mind is not subject to experimental exposure, if all propositions about mind are in principle translatable without residue to propositions about the nervous system, *which is* subject to experimental exposure, then a great deal of mental research can be done in terms of neural research. In general, philosophical consciencism narrows down the extent of academic hermitage. It does this by making research into the nature of one category possible in terms of another category.

There is a growing tendency among some philosophers who

hold the view that when materialism has triumphed and has won victory over idealism, it must, like its victim, disappear or 'wither away' as a philosophy. It is envisaged that this will take place when the classless society is achieved. Marx and Engels regarded materialism as the true form of science and, indeed, held that with the final overthrow of idealism, materialism must have science for its positive content. What is important is not so much that it may not be necessary to stress materialism as a philosophy when idealism is overthrown, but rather that the importance and correctness of materialism will not in any way be diminished in its hour of victory. Some philosophers expect that materialism will then disappear and give way to a philosophy of mind – and that philosophical theory of the mind which is not explicitly prefaced by philosophical materialism will open the door to a new idealism.

Thought without practice is empty, and philosophical consciencism constantly exhibits areas of practical significance, like the one above. If philosophical consciencism initially affirms the absolute and independent existence of matter, and holds matter to be endowed with its pristine objective laws, then philosophical consciencism builds itself by becoming a reflection of the objectivity, in conceptual terms, of the unfolding of matter. When a philosophy so restricts itself to the reflection of the objective unfolding of matter, it also establishes a direct connection between knowledge and action.

This idea of a philosophy as the conceptual image of nature is also found in Spinoza, and, indeed, it is a tenet of rationalism in general. According to Spinoza, at least, the order and connection of ideas is the same as the order and connection of nature. The mistake of the rationalists regarding the connection between philosophy and nature is in their treating philosophy as the blue-print, the strait-jacket for nature, instead of being content with a mere assertion of mutual reflection. If, however, the order and connection of ideas is the same as the order and connection of nature, then according to Spinoza, knowledge of the one order and connection must be knowledge of the other order and connection. Indeed, it can be said that, according to Spinoza, mind is the idea of that whose body is nature.

To the extent that he allows action to be possible, knowledge of the mind can be the direct objective basis of an intervention in nature.

I said earlier on that in spite of the profound cleavage between idealism and materialism, they did not present different inventories of the world. This hardly means, however, that they share the same attitude to the world. They certainly differ in their conception of the nature of the connection between thought and action. In this field, idealism is jejune and grotesquely ineffectual. Materialism is, on the other hand, dynamic and constantly throws up areas of practical significance.

But if philosophical consciencism connects knowledge with action, it is still necessary to inquire whether it conceives this connection as a purely mechanistic one, or whether it makes it susceptible of ethical influence and comment.

It is evident at least that philosophical consciencism cannot issue in a closed set of ethical rules, a set of rules which must apply in any society and at any time. Philosophical consciencism is incapable of this because it is itself based upon a view of matter, as caught in the grip of an inexorable dialectical evolution.

To the extent that materialism issues in egalitarianism on the social plane, it issues in ethics. Egalitarianism is not only political but also ethical; for it implies a certain range of human conduct which is alone acceptable to it. At the same time, because it conceives matter as a plenum of tensions giving rise to dialectical change, it cannot freeze its ethical rules with changelessness. It would be wrong, however, to seek to infer from this that the ethical principles which philosophical consciencism sanctions are at any one time gratuitous and devoid of objective grounding; for even when rules change, they can still be informed, still be governed by the same basic principles in the light of changing social conditions.

It is necessary to understand correctly the relationship between rules and principles. This relationship is similar to that between ideals and institutions and also to that between statutes and by-laws. Statutes, of course, state general principles, they do not make explicit those procedures by means of which they may be carried out and fulfilled. By-laws are an application of such principles. It is obvious that when the conditions in which by-laws operate alter seriously, it could be necessary to amend the by-laws in order that the same statute should continue to be fulfilled. Statutes are not on the same level as by-laws, nor do they imply any *particular* by-laws. It is because they carry no specific implication of particular by-laws, but can be subserved by any one of a whole spectrum of such, that it is possible to amend by-laws, while the statute which they are meant to fulfil suffers no change.

The relationship between ideals and institutions is a similar one. That circumstances change is a truism. For all that, it is significant. For it means that, if ideals must be pursued throughout the changing scenes of life, it may be necessary to modify or replace institutions in order that the same ideals should effectively be served. There are no particular institutions, which, irrespective of local circumstances, are uniquely tied to their ideals. Institutions should be shot through and through with pragmatism.

It is in the same way that principles are related to rules even when they are ethical. The idea that ethical rules can change, and indeed need to change, is one which a little reflection can confirm.

Evidently, even when two societies share the same ethical principles, they may differ in the rules which make the principles effective. Asses were of such overwhelming importance in Israel that God found it necessary to regulate human relations by an ethical rule mentioning them specifically. Thou shalt not covet thy neighbour's ass. If God deigned to give us a similar rule today, he would no doubt forbid us to covet our neighbour's motor-car, hardly his ass. Here God would be giving a new ethical rule, designed at giving effect to an unchanging ethical principle, but taking full account of modern times.

Progress in man's conquest and harnessing of the forces of nature has a profound effect on the content of ethical rules. Some ethical rules fall into abeyance, because the situations in which they take effect lose all likelihood of recurrence; others give way to their opposite, as, for example, when a matriarchal society changes into a patriarchal one, for here many ethical rules arising from the position of the woman will have to give way to those arising from the new position of the man. And yet, the principles standing behind these diverse clusters of ethical rules may remain constant, and identical as between society and society.

According to philosophical consciencism, ethical rules are not permanent but depend on the stage reached in the historical evolution of a society, so however that cardinal principles of egalitarianism are conserved.

A society does not change its ethics by merely changing its rules. To alter its ethics, its principles must be different. Thus, if a capitalist society can become a socialist society, then a capitalist society will have changed its ethics. Any change of ethics constitutes a revolutionary change.

Nevertheless, many times moral rules have changed so startlingly as to give the impression of a revolution in ethics. For example, one can take that profound change in our attitude to offenders for which modern psychology is responsible. Modern psychology brings to our notice relevant facts of whose existence we have no inkling in our dreams. When these new facts change our attitude, moral rules have not necessarily changed. But application of them is withheld, for the new considerations provoke a re-classification of the act involved, and, possibly, bring it under a different ethical rule. In that case, a different moral attitude could become relevant.

Investigations into the psychology of delinquency are a case in point. Such investigations tend by their results to attenuate the acrimony of our moral attitude to delinquents, by compelling us, not admittedly to waive moral rules, but to re-classify delinquent acts.

The cardinal ethical principle of philosophical consciencism is to treat each man as an end in himself and not merely as a means. This is fundamental to all socialist or humanist conceptions of man. It is true that Immanuel Kant also identified this as a cardinal principle of ethics, but whereas he regarded it as an immediate command of reason, we derive it from a materialist viewpoint.

This derivation can be made by way of that egalitarianism which, we have seen, is the social reflection of materialism. Egalitarianism is based on the monistic thesis of materialism. Matter is one even in its different manifestations. If matter is one, it follows that there is a route connecting any two manifestations of matter. This does not mean that between any two manifestations of matter there is a route which does not pass through any third form; the route need not be direct, for it may take one back to the primary form of matter. Dialectical processes are not unilinear, they do not follow just one line, but are ramified. There is a route from any twig of a tree to any other twig, such that the route never leaves the tree. But this does not mean that the twigs all have some one point in common, for it may be necessary to pass to the trunk and join another branch in order to pass from one twig to another. Nevertheless there is this route. The different manifestations of matter are all results of dialectical processes unfolding according to objective laws. There is a determinate process through which every manifestation is derived.

In saying however that there is a route between any two forms of matter, I do not attach the implication that any one form of matter can in fact be derived from any other form, for this may involve the reversal of a process which is irreversible. The upshot of what I mean is the continuity of nature: though the dialectical evolution of matter may lead to culs-de-sac (like the vanished plants and animals of pre-historic days), dialectical evolution contains no hiatuses.

It is the basic unity of matter, despite its varying manifestations, which gives rise to egalitarianism. Basically, man is one, for all men have the same basis and arise from the same evolution according to materialism. This is the objective ground of egalitarianism.

David Hume raised the question that ethical philosophies begin with statements of fact and suddenly seek to base statements of appraisal thereon, without explaining the legitimacy of their inference. If man is basically one, then if action is objectively attentive to this fact, it must be guided by principles. The guiding principles can be stated with such generality that they become autonomous. That is to say, first, that if action is to conform to the objectivity of human unity, then it must be guided by general principles which always keep this objectivity in view, principles which would prevent action from proceeding as if men were basically different. Second, these principles, because they relate to fact, can be stated boldly, as though they were autonomous, like the principle that an individual should not be treated by another merely as a means but always as an end.

If ethical principles are founded on egalitarianism, they must be objective. If ethical principles arise from an egalitarian idea of the nature of man, they must be generalizable, for according to such an idea man is basically one in the sense defined. It is to this non-differential generalization that expression is given in the command to treat each man as an end in himself, and not merely as a means. That is, philosophical consciencism, though it has the same cardinal principle of ethics as Kant, differs from Kant in founding ethics on a philosophical idea of the nature of man. This is what Kant describes as ethics based on anthropology. By anthropology Kant means any study of the nature of man, and he forbids ethics to be based on such a study.

It is precisely this that philosophical consciencism does. It also agrees with the traditional African outlook on many points, and thus fulfils one of the conditions which it sets for itself. In particular, it agrees with the traditional African idea of the absolute and independent existence of matter, the idea of its powers of self-motion in the sense explained, the idea of categorial convertibility, and the idea of the grounding of cardinal principles of ethics in the nature of man.

The traditional African standpoint, of course, accepts the absolute and independent idea of matter. If one takes the philosophy of the African, one finds that in it the absolute and independent existence of matter is accepted. Further, matter is not just dead weight, but alive with forces in tension. Indeed, for the African, everything that exists, exists as a complex of forces in tension. In holding force in tension to be essential to whatever exists, he is, like Thales and like philosophical consciencists, endowing matter with an original power of self-motion, they were endowing it with what matter would need to initiate qualitative and substantial changes.

When a plurality of men exist in society, and it is accepted that each man needs to be treated as an end in himself, not merely as a means, there transpires a transition from ethics to politics. Politics become actual, for institutions need to be created to regulate the behaviour and actions of the plurality of men in society in such a way as to conserve the fundamental ethical principle of the initial worthiness of each individual. Philosophical consciencism consequently adumbrates a political theory and a social-political practice which together seek to ensure that the cardinal principles of ethics are effective.

The social-political practice is directed at preventing the emergence or the solidifying of classes, for in the Marxist conception of class structure, there is exploitation and the subjection of class to class. Exploitation and class-subjection are alike contrary to consciencism. By reason of its egalitarian tenet, philosophical consciencism seeks to promote individual development, but in such a way that the conditions for the development of all become the conditions for the development of each; that is, in such a way that the individual development does not introduce such diversities as to destroy the egalitarian basis. The social-political practice also seeks to co-ordinate social forces in such a way as to mobilize them logistically for the maximum development of society along true egalitarian lines. For this, planned development is essential.

In its political aspect, philosophical consciencism is faced with the realities of colonialism, imperialism, disunity and lack of development. Singly and collectively these four militate against the realization of a social justice based on ideas of true equality.

The first step is to liquidate colonialism wherever it is. In *Towards Colonial Freedom* I stated that it is the aim of colonial governments to treat their colonies as producers of raw materials, and at the same time as the dumping-ground of the manufactured goods of foreign industrialists and foreign capitalists. I have always believed that the basis of colonialism is economic, but the solution of the colonial problem lies in political action, in a fierce and constant struggle for emancipation as an indispensable first step towards securing economic independence and integrity.

I said earlier on that consciencism regards matter as a plenum of forces in tension; and that in its dialectical aspect, it holds categorial conversion to be possible by a critical disposition of matter. This gives us a clue how to analyse the fact of colonialism, not only in Africa, but indeed everywhere. It also gives us a clue how to defeat it.

In a colonial situation, there are forces which tend to promote colonialism, to promote those political ties by means of which a colonialist country binds its colonies to itself with the primary object of furthering her economic advantages. Colonialism requires exertion, and much of that exertion is taken up by the combat of progressive forces, forces which seek to negate this oppressive enterprise of greedy individuals and classes by means of which an egotistical imposition of the strong is made upon the weak.

Just as the placid appearance of matter only disguises the tension of forces underlying that appearance, like the bow of Heraclitus, so in a colonial territory, an opposition of reactionary and revolutionary forces can nevertheless give an impression of final and acquiescent subjugation. But just as a quality can be changed by quantitative (measurable) changes of a critical nature in matter, so this acquiescent impression can be obliterated by a change in the relation of the social forces. These opposing sets of forces are dynamic, in the sense that they seek and tend to establish some social condition. One may therefore refer to them by the name of action in order to make their dynamic nature explicit. In that case, one may say that in a colonial situation positive action and negative action can be discerned. Positive action will represent the sum of those forces seeking social justice in terms of the destruction of oligarchic exploitation and oppression. Negative action will correspondingly represent the sum of those forces tending to prolong colonial subjugation and exploitation. Positive action is revolutionary and negative action is reactionary.

It ought to be recognized at the outset that the introduced terms of positive and negative action are abstractions. But the ground for them is in social reality. It is quite possible by means of statistical analysis to discover the ways in which positive action and negative action are related in any given society. The statistical analysis will be of such facts as production, distribution, income, etc. Any such analysis must reveal one of three possible situations. Positive action may exceed negative action, or negative action may exceed positive action, or they may form an unstable equilibrium.

In a colonial situation, negative action undoubtedly outweighs positive action. In order that true independence should be won, it is necessary that positive action should come to overwhelm negative action. Admittedly, a semblance of true independence is possible without this specific relation. When this happens, we say that neo-colonialism has set in, for neo-colonialism is a guise adopted by negative action in order to give the impression that it has been overcome by positive action. Neo-colonialism is negative action playing possum.

In order to forestall this, it is necessary for positive action to be backed by a mass party, and qualitatively to improve this mass so that by education and an increase in its degree of consciousness, its aptitude for positive action becomes heightened. We can therefore say that in a colonial territory, positive action must be backed by a mass party, complete with its instruments of education. This was why the Convention People's Party of Ghana developed from an early stage its education wing, workers' wing, farmers' wing, youth wing, women's wing, etc. In this way, the people received constant political education, their self-awareness was increased and such a self-image was formed as ruthlessly excluded colonialism in all its guises. It is also in the backing of millions of members and supporters, united by a common radical purpose, that the revolutionary character of the Convention People's Party consists, and not merely in the piquancy of its programmes. Its mass and national support made it possible to think in realistic terms of instituting changes of a fundamental nature in the social hotch-potch bequeathed by colonialism.

A people's parliamentary democracy with a one-party system

is better able to express and satisfy the common aspirations of a nation as a whole, than a multiple-party parliamentary system, which is in fact only a ruse for perpetuating, and covers up, the inherent struggle between the 'haves' and the 'have-nots'.

In order that a territory should acquire the nominal attributes of independence, it is of course not necessary that positive action should exceed negative action. When a colonialist country sees the advance of positive action, it unfailingly develops a policy of containment, a policy whereby it seeks to check this advance and limit it. This policy often takes the form of conferences and protracted constitutional reforms.

Containment is, however, accepted by the colonialist country only as a second best. What it would really like to do is to roll back positive action. It is when it is assured of the impossibility of rolling back the billows of history that it applies the policy of containment, that it tries to limit the achievement of progress by devising frivolous reforms. The colonialist country seeks to divert positive action into channels which are harmless to it.

To do this it resorts to diverse subtle means. Having abandoned direct violence, the colonialist country imparts a deceptive orientation to the negative forces in its subject territory. These negative forces become the political wolf masquerading in sheep's clothing, they join the clamour for independence, and are accepted in good faith by the people. It is then that like a wasting disease they seek from the inside to infest, corrupt, pervert and thwart the aspirations of the people.

The people, the body and the soul of the nation, the final sanction of political decisions, and the inheritors of sovereignty, cannot be fooled for long. Quick on the scent, they ferret out these Janus-faced politicians who run with the hare and hunt with the hounds. They turn away from them. Once this colonialist subterfuge is exposed, and the minion accomplices discredited, the colonial power has no option but to acknowledge the independence of the people. By its very next act, however, it seeks without grace to neutralize this same independence by fomenting discontent and disunity; and, finally, by arrant ingratiation and wheedling it

attempts to disinherit the people and constitute itself their conscience and their will, if not their voice and their arm. Political
decisions, just as they were before independence was won, lose
their reference to the welfare of the people, and serve once again
the well-being and security of the erstwhile colonial power and the
clique of self-centred politicians.

Any oblique attempt of a foreign power to thwart, balk, corrupt
or otherwise pervert the true independence of a sovereign people is
neo-colonialist. It is neo-colonialist because it seeks, notwithstanding the acknowledged sovereignty of a people, to subordinate their
interests to those of a foreign power.

A colonialist country can in fact offer independence to a people,
not with the intention which such an act might be thought to imply,
but in the hope that the positive and progressive forces thus
appeased and quietened, the people might be exploited with
greater serenity and comfort.

Neo-colonialism is a greater danger to independent countries
than is colonialism. Colonialism is crude, essentially overt, and apt
to be overcome by a purposeful concert of national effort. In neo-
colonialism, however, the people are divided from their leaders
and, instead of providing true leadership and guidance which is
informed at every point by the ideal of the general welfare, leaders
come to neglect the very people who put them in power and
incautiously become instruments of suppression on behalf of the
neo-colonialists.

It is far easier for the proverbial camel to pass through the
needle's eye, hump and all, than for an erstwhile colonial administration to give sound and honest counsel of a *political* nature to
its liberated territory. To allow a foreign country, especially one
which is loaded with economic interests in our continent, to tell us
what *political* decisions to take, what *political* courses to follow, is
indeed for us to hand back our independence to the oppressor on a
silver platter.

Likewise, since the motivation of colonialism, whatever protean
forms it may take, is well and truly economic, colonialism itself
being but the institution of political bonds fastening colonies to a

colonialist country, with the primary object of the metropolitan economic advantages, it is essential that a liberated territory should not bind her economy to that of the ousted rulers. The liberation of a people institutes principles which enjoin the recognition and destruction of imperialistic domination, whether it is political, economic, social or cultural. To destroy imperialistic domination in these forms, political, economic, social and cultural action must always have reference to the needs and nature of the liberated territory, and it is from these needs and nature that the action must derive authenticity. Unless this self-reference is religiously maintained, a liberated territory will welcome with open arms the very foe which it has sought to destroy at cost of terrible suffering.

The true welfare of a people does not admit of compromise. If we compromise on the true interest of our people, the people must one day judge us, for it is with their effort and their sacrifice, with their forbearance and their denial, that independence is won. Independence once won, it is possible to rule against the erstwhile colonial power, but it is not really possible to rule against the wish and interest of the people.

The people are the backbone of positive action. It is by the people's effort that colonialism is routed, it is by the sweat of the people's brow that nations are built. The people are the reality of national greatness. It is the people who suffer the depredations and indignities of colonialism, and the people must not be insulted by dangerous flirtations with neo-colonialism.

There is a fundamental law of the evolution of matter to higher forms. This evolution is dialectical. And it is also the fundamental law of society. It is out of tension that being is born. Becoming is a tension, and being is the child of that tension of opposed forces and tendencies.

Just as in the physical universe, since the moving object is always impressed upon by external forces, any motion is in fact a resultant, so in society every development, every progressive motion, is a resultant of unharmonious forces, a resultant, a triumph of positive action over negative action.

This triumph must be accompanied by knowledge. For in the way that the process of natural evolution can be aided by human intervention based upon knowledge, so social evolution can be helped along by political intervention based upon knowledge of the laws of social development. Political action aimed at speeding up social evolution is of the nature of a catalyst.

The need for such a catalyst is created by the fact that natural evolution is always wasteful. It takes place at the cost of massive loss of life and at the cost of extreme anguish. Evolution speeded by scientific knowledge is prompter, and represents an economy of material. In the same way, the catalysis which political action introduces into social evolution represents an economy of time, life and talent.

Without positive action, a colonial territory cannot be truly liberated. It is doomed to creep in its petty pace from day to day towards the attainment of a sham independence that turns to dust, independence which is shot through and through with the supreme interest of an alien power. To achieve true liberation, positive action must begin with an objective analysis of the situation which it seeks to change. Such an analysis I attempted in *Towards Colonial Freedom*. Positive action must, furthermore, seek an alignment of all the forces of progress and, by marshalling them, confront the negative forces. It must at the same time anticipate and contain its own inner contradictions, for, though positive action unites those forces of a situation which are, in regard to a specific purpose, progressive, many of these forces will contain tendencies which are in other respects reactionary.

Hence, when positive action resorts to an alignment of forces, it creates in itself seams at which this alignment might fall apart. It is essential that positive action should in its dialectical evolution anticipate this seminal disintegration and discover a way of containing the future schismatic tendencies, a way of nipping fragmentation in the bud as colonialism begins to reel and totter under the frontal onslaught of positive action.

But even with colonialism worsted, positive action cannot relent, for it is at about this time that the schismatic tendencies referred to ripen. Besides, political independence, though worth while in itself, is still only a means to the fuller redemption and realization of a people. When independence has been gained, positive action requires a new orientation away from the sheer destruction of colonialism and towards national reconstruction.

It is indeed in this address to national reconstruction that positive action faces its gravest dangers. The cajolement, the wheedlings, the seductions and the Trojan horses of neo-colonialism must be stoutly resisted, for neo-colonialism is a latter-day harpy, a monster which entices its victims with sweet music.

In order to be able to carry out this resistance to neo-colonialism at every point, positive action requires to be armed with an ideology, an ideology which, vitalizing it and operating through a mass party shall equip it with a regenerative concept of the world and life, forge for it a strong continuing link with our past and offer to it an assured bond with our future. Under the searchlight of an ideology, every fact affecting the life of a people can be assessed and judged, and neo-colonialism's detrimental aspirations and sleights of hand will constantly stand exposed.

In order that this ideology should be comprehensive, in order that it should light up every aspect of the life of our people, in order that it should affect the total interest of our society, establishing a continuity with our past, it must be socialist in form and in content and be embraced by a mass party.

And yet, socialism in Africa today tends to lose its objective content in favour of a distracting terminology and in favour of a general confusion. Discussion centres more on the various conceivable types of socialism than upon the need for socialist development. More is surely required than a mere reaction against a policy of domination. Independence is of the people; it is won by the people for the people. That independence is of the people is admitted by every enlightened theory of sovereignty. That it is won by the people is to be seen in the successes of mass movements everywhere. That it is won for the people follows from their ownership of sovereignty. The people have not mastered their independence until it has been given a national and social content and purpose that will generate their well-being and uplift.

The socialism of a liberated territory is subject to a number of principles if independence is not to be alienated from the people. When socialism is true to its purpose, it seeks a connection with the egalitarian and humanist past of the people before their social evolution was ravaged by colonialism; it seeks from the results of colonialism those elements (like new methods of industrial production and economic organization) which can be adapted to serve the interest of the people; it seeks to contain and prevent the spread of those anomalies and domineering interests created by the capitalist habit of colonialism; it reclaims the psychology of the people, erasing the 'colonial mentality' from it; and it resolutely defends the independence and security of the people. In short, socialism recognizes dialectic, the possibility of creation from forces which are opposed to one another; it recognizes the creativity of struggle, and, indeed, the necessity of the operation of forces to any change. It also embraces materialism and translates this into social terms of equality.

CHAPTER 5

SET THEORETIC TERMS

S O ALERT can positive action be, alert to all negative possibilities, and prompt under the guidance of an ideology to deal with these possibilities, that the course of positive action can be mapped out in set theoretic terms. For this, a minimum number of initial symbols are necessary.

Let Pa	represent	the positive action in an individual
Na	,,	the negative action in an individual
pa	,,	the positive action in a society
na	,,	the negative action in a society
$>$	,,	is greater than
$<$	,,	is less than
g	,,	a territory
$(na>pa)g$	,,	a territory in which negative action is greater than positive action
$(pa>na)g$	,,	a territory in which positive action is greater than negative action
$col.g$	,,	g is a colony
$lib.g$	,,	g is liberated
(na)	,,	for all na
(pa)	,,	for all pa
(g)	,,	for all g
$\exists$	,,	there is a
Gi	,,	a liberated territory
$\rightarrow$	,,	if then
$\leftarrow\rightarrow$	,,	if and only if
D	,,	dialectical moment in general. It defines a factor which changes the relation between pa and na, by converting pa greater than na to na greater than pa, or vice versa

Let d represent a measure of dialectical moment as defined above

$\nearrow$	,,	on the increase
$\searrow$	,,	on the decrease
m	,,	philosophical materialism
C	,,	philosophical consciencism in general
cg	,,	philosophical consciencism as elaborated by the conditions of g and the experience and consciousness of its people
O	,,	zero
Lm	,,	limit of
ξ	,,	a negligible quantity
UGi	,,	Gi is united
$+$	,,	jointly with
p	,,	index of development
$=$	,,	equal to
ϕ	,,	the relation of forces required for development
Σ	,,	sum of
S	,,	socialism in general
Sg	,,	socialism in the conditions of g
$\propto$	,,	an optimum zone for development
$S\propto$	,,	socialism in the conditions of $\propto$

I have said that a colony is any territory in which the interests of the people are alienated from them and subjected to those of a group distinct from the people of the territory itself. It follows that a colony may be externally or internally subjected. When the interests of the people are subjected to those of a group outside the territory itself, it is said to be externally subjected. When the interests are subjected to those of a class in the sense of Marx within the territory itself, it is said to be internally subjected.

The Union of South Africa would be an example of an internally subjected colony. It is obvious that such a colony enjoys the legal attributes of independence.

Colony is an economic-political term, not a legal one.

It is possible for the same territory to be both internally and externally subjected. Southern Rhodesia is such a colony. In either type of colony, however, negative action is essentially greater than positive action. Hence the symbolic representation of a territory g which is a colony is

(i) $col.g. \longleftrightarrow (na > pa)g$

Since, according to philosophical consciencism in its embracing of philosophical dialectical materialism, a change can only result from an operation of forces, in order to liberate a colony a dialectical moment needs to be introduced in $(na > pa)g$ to transform it to $(pa > na)g$. Hence, a liberated territory arises under the condition

(ii) $lib.g \longleftrightarrow [D(na > pa)g \rightarrow (pa > na)g]$

In this formula, it is also said that the dialectical moment must be sufficient for the transformation of $(na > pa)$ to $(pa > na)$.

And since the intention of this dialectical moment is to produce the relation $(pa > na)$, another formula arises thus:

(iii) $D(na > pa) \rightarrow pa \nearrow + na \searrow O$

Since $D(na > pa) \rightarrow pa \nearrow + na \searrow O$ there is always a dialectical

moment such that

(iv) $d(na > pa)g \rightarrow (pa > na)g$

This in its general form is

(v) $(pa)(na)(g) \exists d [d(na > pa)g \rightarrow (pa > na)g]$

to give us an existence theorem. But, equally, the following obtain:

(vi) $D(pa > na) \rightarrow na \nearrow + pa \searrow O$

Hence there is always a dialectical moment such that

(vii) $d(pa > na)g \rightarrow (na > pa)g$

This in turn can be universalized as

(viii) $(pa)(na)(g) \exists d [d(pa > na)g \rightarrow (na > pa)g]$

That is, in any territory, liberation can be won (v) or lost (viii). This is why every liberated territory must keep on increasing its positive action if it would remain liberated. In particular, in order to thwart neo-colonialism, positive action requires to be maintained in preponderance over negative action.

By successive instantiation, we obtain the following deductions:

$$(pa)(na)(g) \exists d [d(na > pa)g \rightarrow (pa > na)g]$$
$$(na)(g) \exists d [d(na > pa)g \rightarrow (pa > na)g]$$
$$(g) \exists d [d(na > pa)g \rightarrow (pa > na)g]$$
$$\exists d [d(na > pa)g \rightarrow (pa > na)g]$$

It will be observed from the formula (iii) according to which

$$D(na > pa) \rightarrow pa^{\nearrow} + na_{\searrow O} \qquad \text{that the decrease of negative action}$$

secured by introducing a dialectical moment into $(na > pa)$ approaches zero. But not even in the limit does na quite attain to $\searrow O$

zero, for according to philosophical consciencism every situation is a plenum of forces in tension. Hence, negative action cannot disappear completely but could only become a negligible quantity. I therefore put down as

(ix) $Lm\, D(na > pa) \rightarrow pa^{\nearrow} + \xi na$

The above formulae are subject to a rule of substitution, which enables us to substitute constants on variables, and a rule of detachment which enables us, granted an antecedent, to assert a consequence. Thus, if b is the name of a colony, we can obtain the following derivation:

$$col\ g \longleftrightarrow (na > pa)g \ldots \text{(i)}$$
$$col\ b \longleftrightarrow (na > pa)b \ldots \text{rule of substitution}$$

By this rule, the general condition for a colony is applied to every individual colony.

Again, we may obtain the following derivation:

$$(pa)(na)(g)\ \exists\, d\,[d(na > pa)g \rightarrow (pa > na)g] \ldots \text{a}$$
$$(pa)(na)\ \exists\, d\,[d(na > pa)g \rightarrow (pa > na)g] \ldots \text{b}$$
$$(na)\ \exists\, d\,[d(na > pa)g \rightarrow (pa > na)g] \ldots \text{c}$$
$$\exists\, d\,[d(na > pa)g \rightarrow (pa > na)g] \ldots \text{d}$$
$$d(na > pa)g \rightarrow (pa > na)g \ldots \text{e}$$
$$d(na > pa)g \qquad\qquad \ldots \text{f}$$
$$\therefore\ (pa > na)\ \text{rule of detachment} \ldots \text{g.}$$

This derivation, according to rules analogous to those of the predicate calculus, shows that if a freedom fighter can by increasing positive action introduce a sufficient dialectical moment in $(na > pa)g$, he can be sure of winning independence.

Alternatively,

$$(pa)(na)(g)\ \exists\, d\,[d(na > pa)g \rightarrow (pa > na)g] \ \ldots\ \text{(a)}$$
$$lib.g \longleftrightarrow D(na > pa)g \rightarrow (pa > na)g \ldots \text{(ii)} \ldots \text{(b)}$$
$$\therefore\,[D(na > pa)g \rightarrow (pa > na)g] \rightarrow lib.g \ldots \text{(c)}$$

from (ii), (iii), (iv), (c)

$$[d(na > pa)g \rightarrow (pa > na)g] \rightarrow lib.g \ \ldots\ \text{(d)}$$

but from (a) $(na)(g)\ \exists\, d\,[d(na > pa)g \rightarrow (pa > na)g]$. (e)

" " (e) $(g)\ \exists\, d\,[d(na > pa)g \rightarrow (pa > na)g]$. (f)

" " (f) $\exists\, d\,[d(na > pa)g \rightarrow (pa > na)g]$. (g)

" " (g) $d(na > pa)g \rightarrow (pa > na)g$. (h)

from (d) and (h) $lib.g$.

But independence does not automatically bring that unity of purpose required for maintaining it. Indeed, a reaction could quickly set in, for just as a liberated territory can be produced by the application of $D(na > pa)$, so a neo-colonized territory can be produced by the application of $D(pa > na)$. Further and sustained positive action is required to consolidate independence, and to raise a liberated territory to the level of a united nation. Hence,

$$\text{(x)} \quad UGi \longleftrightarrow (p\overset{\nearrow}{a} + na) \\ \qquad\qquad\qquad\qquad \searrow_{O \ Gi}$$

In a newly independent territory, though unity might be produced by this increase of positive action over negative action, this unity will not necessarily be secure from the ravages of negative action. On the contrary, reactionary forces plunge their battering ram into the heart of its foundations. In order to stem and reverse this advance of reaction, a union of liberated territories is called for.

Let G_1 to Gk represent liberated territories in a geographical zone; then a union of G_1 to Gk, designated as $UG_{1...k}$ is required to maintain this unity and preserve independence. To produce this unity in a zone of liberated territories, G_1 to Gk, positive action needs to be increased in them conjointly. Hence,

$$\text{(xi)} \quad UG_{1...k} \longleftrightarrow (p\overset{\nearrow}{a} + na) \\ \qquad\qquad\qquad\qquad\qquad \searrow_{O \ G_{1...k}}$$

But a qualitative distinction needs to be introduced into the formula (xi). A union of liberated territories could unfortunately be formed for reactionary purposes, and for the aiding and abetting of neo-colonialist interests. Hence the progressive union of liberated territories, for example, a union of African States, might be better represented as

$$\text{(xii)} \quad U \ G_{1...k} \longleftrightarrow (p\overset{\nearrow}{a} + na) \\ \qquad\qquad\qquad\qquad\qquad \searrow_{O \ G_{1...k}}$$

or, more analytically

$$(\text{xiii}) \quad U_{pa}\, G_{1\ldots k} \longleftrightarrow [(\overset{\nearrow}{pa} + na) + (\overset{\nearrow}{pa} + na) + \ldots$$
$$\searrow O\, G_1 \qquad \searrow O\, G_2$$

$$\ldots + (\overset{\nearrow}{pa} + na) + (\overset{\nearrow}{pa} + na)Gk]$$
$$\searrow OG_{k-1} \qquad \searrow O$$

We have seen that for purposes of true development, a liberated territory must embrace philosophical consciencism. In its materialist aspect, philosophical consciencism preserves a humanist egalitarianism. The philosophical materialism which forms a part of consciencism accommodates dialectic, and holds it to be the efficient cause of all change. In order that development may not be gibbous, philosophical consciencism insists that account must be taken of the material conditions of the territory involved, as account must also be taken of the experience and consciousness of the people whose redemption is sought. A people can only be redeemed by lifting themselves up, as it were, by the strings of their boots. In these circumstances development must be socialist. It is only a socialist scheme of development which can ensure that a society is redeemed, that the general welfare is honestly pursued, that autonomy rests with the society as a whole and not in part, that the experience and consciousness of the people are not ravaged and raped. It is only a socialist scheme of development that can meet the passionate objectivity of philosophical consciencism.

We may symbolize the relation of forces required for development as ϕ. In that case we obtain a formula:

$$(\text{xiv}) \quad \phi \longleftrightarrow m + C + D,$$

such that ϕ is secured only in the presence of philosophical materialism, dialectic and consciencism. It will be seen at once that this formula contains a redundancy, for m is a part of C, and so is a belief in D. This redundant formulation has, however, a psychological aspect which is valuable in making the necessity for m and D both explicit and unmistakable.

I have argued that the condition for optimum development which shall be humanist is socialist through and through. If we make S represent socialism, then we can obtain an analytic formula as follows:

$$(xv) \quad S \longleftrightarrow \phi + UGi$$

This short formula summarizes a number of weighty truths, namely, that there is socialism if and only if there is the conjoint presence of philosophical materialism, philosophical consciencism, dialectic and national unity, in a liberated territory. It is essential that socialism should include overriding regard to the experience and consciousness of a people, for if it does not do so, it will be serving an idea and not a people. It will generate a contradiction. It will become dogmatic. It will shed its materialist and realist basis. It will become a fanaticism, an obscurantism, an alienator of human happiness.

When we talk of socialism in Africa, therefore, we really do intend to include as part of socialism an overriding regard to our actual material conditions, an overriding regard to our experience and our consciousness.

Appropriately therefore a general formula arises thus:

$$(xvi) \quad S \longleftrightarrow m + C + D + UGi$$

Here, m is a constant, for the theses of philosophical materialism are constant. C, however, stands for philosophical consciencism in general and not for the actual content which it should have in a territory g if it is to pay attention to the material conditions of the territory, and the experience and consciousness of its people. D, too, stands for a dialectical moment in general, but the actual form and content of this moment depends on the situation which it seeks to change, and the resources which, in a particular case, it has for bringing about the desirable change. D is therefore a variable. UGi, because it is a function of d, pa and na, is also a variable, because dependent. It is the variable nature of the parameters of formula (xv) which determines its generality.

But the formula at the same time gives a clue to the form it should take in any particular territory, g. The following formula results:

(xvii) $Sg \longleftrightarrow m + cg + d + U \, lib.g$

and for an optimum zone $\propto$, it has the form:

(xviii) $S \propto \longleftrightarrow m + c \propto + d + U \, lib. \propto$

If b be the name of a particular territory, then we obtain

(xix) $S_b \longleftrightarrow m + c_b + d + U \, lib.b.$

Hence, in order that socialism should be applicable in a country, the country must be liberated; it must enjoy unity; it must embrace philosophical materialism; it must have a specific philosophical consciencism holding its general nature in common, but expressing its individuality through the actual material conditions of the territory for which it is formulated, and through the experience and consciousness of the people of that territory; it must apply suitable and adequate dialectical moments, expressed through positive action, wielded through a mass party.

In order to liberate a territory, an increase of positive action over negative action must be obtained by the introduction of a dialectical moment. This dialectical moment can be introduced by joining together the forces of positive action in one mass political party, educating the people, explaining to them the evil nature of colonialism, that is, analysing their experience and giving them a greater awareness of this experience through workers' sections, farmers' sections, youth sections, women's sections, newspapers and other implements of party organization. To unite the liberated territory, the mass political party must be further developed to the size of a popular movement. The policies of development then need to accord with the theses of philosophical materialism, and they must be subject to philosophical consciencism, showing a sensitivity to the material conditions and experience of the people.

The analytic form of (xvi) – (xix) reveals that socialism cannot be dogmatic in its *specific* provisions, for it contains constant and variable elements. In principle, socialism remains the same and pure; in application it is realistic and scientific.

Caution is supremely necessary here. A clever and unscrupulous neo-colonialism can pervert and corrupt this relativist aspect of specific socialism and use it in fact to re-colonize a people. It is essential that socialism in its specific form should at every point and every level be justified only by reference to *socialist* general principles. Specific socialism can only be an *instantiation* of the general formula, no more. The people should therefore not be betrayed under the guise of relating socialism to their actual conditions.

At this point, I shall give further elucidation to the concept of positive action. I have already pointed out that positive action as a lever towards independence is related to a mass party and the political education, unity of purpose and action which it can impart to a people. Positive action as a quantity could therefore vary with people, their degree of consciousness, and their degree of mobilization for progress. The people are however not conscious or mobilized apart from the consciousness and mobilization of individuals. *pa* may therefore be said to be the sum of the positive action, *Pa*, contained in individuals associated with a mass organization. Therefore,

$$(\text{xx}) \quad pa = Pa_1 + Pa_2 + \ldots + Pa_{k-1} + Pa_k = \Sigma Pa_{1 \ldots k}$$

Similarly, *na* represents the sum of the negative action, *Na*, of the individuals in a society to the extent that it is organized and concerted. Hence,

$$(\text{xxi}) \quad na = Na_1 + Na_2 + \ldots + Na_{k-1} + Na_k = \Sigma Na_{1 \ldots k}$$

Thus, both *pa* and *na* are revealed as functions.

Since all the steps taken towards a genuine development of a liberated territory involve a relation of positive action to negative action, the index of development, p, may be defined thus:

(xxii) $\quad P = \dfrac{pa}{na}$

As na never completely disappears, however closely it approaches O, p can never become infinite, but at its peak has the following equivalence:

(xxiii) $\quad P = \dfrac{pa}{\xi\, na}$

P is therefore asymptotic towards infinity at its peak. It is increased by increasing pa and decreasing na. In practice, however, na is never negligible and $\xi\, na$ is never attained.

But though $\xi\, na$ is never achieved, the index of development can rise as pa rises and na decreases. If this is what is required according to the equation for the index of development, then it can be

secured by the same leverage as brings about $(pa + na)$. The intensi-

$$\left(pa \overset{\nearrow}{+} na\right)_{\searrow O}$$

fication of the dialectical moment which produces independence will raise the index of development. A greater positive action therefore emerges as the key to development along socialist lines. That is, for socialist development, the socialist conscience of the people must be enhanced through education and party activity. The forces of positive action, political, economic and cultural, need to be mobilized and streamlined for progress.

This requires an increase in the number of people contributing to positive action and an improvement in the quality of their contribution. This requires a greater space $\propto$, achieved through positive unity as defined in formula (xiii), and it creates an optimum zone of self-induced development.

I should like at this point to revert to a general feature of philosophical consciencism. Philosophical consciencism is a general philosophy which admits of application to any country. But it is especially applicable to colonies and newly independent and developing countries. In the case of Africa, by means of the foregoing set theoretic methods the necessity of a union of independent African states is established, a union integrated by socialism, without which our hard-won independence may yet be perverted and negated by a new colonialism.

INDEX